SPECTRE DETECTORS INVESTIGATE BISHOP AUCKLAND

My name is Elaine Kelly and I am the lead investigator for Spectre Detectors, one of the North East's most hard working team of paranormal investigators. We work extremely hard to bring you evidence of the spirit world, watching and listening to hours of footage from each investigation.

But let me tell you a little bit about myself and how I started investigating the paranormal.

I was born in County Durham and have lived in a little mining village called Coundon, which is just outside of Bishop Auckland, for all of my life. I went to school At King James 1st and spent nearly every Friday night doing a pub crawl around the town. Bishop Auckland really was the place to be on a night out.

On a Saturday it was also the place to go for shopping, anything from Clothing to a musical instrument. You had many of the main high street names in the town, along with the Co-op which was a huge department store. Doggart's was also a main shop for the town but I cant remember it.

In my 30's I started to work in a local supermarket working nightshift and this was when I became more aware of the spirit world. I saw things that made me want to learn more about the afterlife so started to go to spiritualist churches, eventually joining in with awareness classes. I started to experience more of the spirit world. I started to see spirit, would often hear spirit calling my name and I sensed spirit around me.

I could walk into a building and tell immediately if there was a spirit present. I could also tell people if anything dramatic had happened in a building and exactly where in the building it was, just by walking into the room and feeling the shift in energy.

It's through working nightshift that I first met Bev. We were both aware of the hauntings within the store but were both surprisingly comfortable with the spirits that resided there.

Developing my own gifts made me want to learn more about the spirit world. I believed in mediumship and what most of them said, but I wanted to gather solid evidence. I stopped going to the spiritualist church for various reasons, some of them being family commitments but mostly because I felt that I was expected to give messages and train to work on the rostrum. I didn't feel that this was for me and that the spirit world had a different path planned out for me. And I was right.

After about 4 years of working together (back in 2011), Bev and I decided to do a paranormal night. Equipped with only a Handy Cam, voice recorder and a K2 meter we investigated one of the most haunted building within County Durham. Looking back, we really didn't have much of a clue about how to investigate a haunted building. But what we did know about was being respectful, never to provoke and to do as much protection prayers as we could. That night we caught some amazing EVP's of a man moaning!

That was the beginning of Spectre Detectors. I had to come up with a name because whenever I booked a venue they asked for a group name. I wanted a name that rolled off the tongue, and that wasn't already in use.

About 5 years later, I approached a popular local medium about doing a special event. We didn't really organise events with mediums as we like to use our own gifts, but I thought it would be a great way of getting known. I booked the venue where our journey began and the event went brilliantly. She had brought some of her students with her and I'm so pleased to say that most of them are still with the team today.

We have always shared our evidence and footage on our social media pages, but someone suggested that I write a book about our experiences. I wasn't really sure about it at first, but thought it would be a great way of documenting our findings. So, I wrote Entering the darkness – a paranormal quest. It was very rough around the edges, as I had no previous experience in writing. I wrote the book in a diary style, just as it happened, but didn't really include the full spirit box sessions. But I learned as I went along and changed things. The style is still very much the same, but I have included everything. A have also started to do the history of the place and do some research too, which is the hardest part. When we are talking to spirit, they don't tell you every detail, you have to try your best to make the pieces fit. Very rarely do you get Christian and surnames. It's usually one or the other.

I also wanted to point out that investigating the paranormal isn't something to be taken lightly. I have been held by the throat, punched in the side, locked in rooms (many times), and have even had spirit use my body in trance. You must protect yourselves at all times, never provoke, don't take unnecessary risks or go off on your own. This doesn't mean that you can't do lone vigils, but always have someone at the other side of the door or use a walkie talkie. Never ask spirit to do something that you aren't prepared for, because the worst thing to do is to show fear or to panic.

But please do not think that dealing with the spirit world has to be scary. If it is done correctly and responsibly, it can be a very uplifting experience. I hope that you enjoy this book and can take some hints and tips from them. The other books in the series are Entering the darkness – a paranormal quest, Spectre Detectors – uncovering the truth, Spectre Detectors - Following the Ripper, Spirits of the North, Ghostly gems of Jedburgh, The Hauntings of Bishop Auckland, Voices From the Past. The Ghosts of Bishop Auckland and surrounding areas, The Hauntings of County Durham, The Ghosts of Gilesgate and Durham, The Ghosts of the North Sea Coast, Spectre Detectors Investigate Hartlepool and Seaton Carew, The Hauntings of Darlington, The Curse of Mary Ann Cotton, Discovering Durham's Dark Past, Spectre Detectors Investigate Newcastle and Hexham, Spectre Detectors Investigate Spennymoor, Croxdale and Tudhoe, Spectre Detectors Investigate The Sportsman's Inn and Spectre Detectors Investigate The Dun Cow.

I have been interviewed many times on radio – The Paranormal Chronicles and The Unexplained with Howard Hughes, been in the local and nation press and have been featured in many paranormal magazines both here and overseas. In May 2022 I was featured on TalkTV.

Following on from the success of The Hauntings of Bishop Auckland and The Ghosts of Bishop Auckland, this book is about the investigations that we have done in and around Bishop Auckland over the last twelve months.

We have tried to research the information that we were given but this is really difficult. Spirit don't give you an awful lot to go on and information wasn't really logged or registered anywhere from such a long time ago. We can never be 100% sure that the information we have been given is correct but we have given people who could possibly link to the spirits we have encountered. If anyone has any information regarding any details in the book, please get in touch, we would love to hear from you.

Our email address is spectredetectors@yahoo.co.uk

Facebook is
https://www.facebook.com/spectredetectors/

I hope you enjoy the book, please just enjoy it for what it is. We aren't trying to convince anyone that the spirit world exists but if we could just open your mind slightly to the possibility, then I'm happy.

Spectre Detectors Investigate Bishop Auckland includes some buildings that are off the beaten track. We start the story at Fore Bondgate where we have investigated Gregg Bros and Labyrinth, then visit Waldron street where we have investigate The Welcome, then onto Peel Street where we have investigated Cre8ive Graphics.

GREGG BROS

Whilst thinking about fabulous venues to feature in our 3rd book about Bishop Auckland, I thought I would contact Gregg Bros as I knew that they had been in Bishop Auckland for many years. I contacted the shop and they were very welcoming and were very intrigued about what stories the shop would have to say.

We went along to do a private investigation in June 2021 and met Debbie and Vicky. They didn't really know what would be happening during the evening so we spent a short while explaining what would happen during the evening.

We travelled very light, only taking a Handy Cam, voice recorder, table for tipping, K2 meters, full spectrum cameras, thermal imaging camera, and a few trigger objects, including the pendulums that were on a stand.

Earlier that day I had seen a rainbow on my bathroom door, and I usually associate that with Mary Ann Cotton or the children linked to her. I knew that there was a chance that someone linked to her would come through that night but didn't really think too much about it as we started the investigation.

I set up the Handy Cam on a stand along with the voice recorder. We set the doll and poppy bear on the floor, and set up a motion sensor in the doorway of the back room. I did this because as I was having a look around, it felt like we were being watched and it was as if I had walked through a spirit stood there.

We said the prayer and all took a seat, just taking in the energy of the room, which had become palpable. You could see the energy swirling around is all and I picked up a K2 meter and inspected the room. The K2 was on amber at the lower half of the room but as I went higher towards the ceiling it dropped. It was like someone of my height was stood near to me but everywhere I went, it went too.

I explained to Debbie how the K2 worked and that It picked up electromagnetic energy which can be caused by spirit along with normal electrical items. Hannah also said that the room was full of energy. I told Debbie that spirit could communicate using the K2 meter.

I asked if anyone was picking up on any spirits. Hannah said she had a girl called Molly. I was picking up on a stroke condition but didn't know if it was a man or woman. Shayna felt like she had a tight chest. A fly had gone into the fly killer and we talked about it and caught a child saying 'catchy'. I said that I was recording on the Handy Cam.

Debbie wanted to tell us a bit about the Gregg family but I stopped her and asked her to give me the information afterwards. Debbie said that she rented the shop off Anne Gregg and Bev said that the shop was very different in the past. The talked about it having sawdust on the floor and we caught an EVP on Handy Cam saying 'Gregg'. I was still trying to work out why the K2 meter was going off. Hannah said it was because the shop was full of energy. I said we would see if we could pick anything up before I put the portal on.

I asked spirit to knock on something for me. Debbie went into the kitchen to turn off the refrigerator and accidentally set off the motion sensor, scaring herself to death. Immediately after she knocked it off a man was caught on voice recorder saying 'oh'. I was still picking up on a person whom I felt had suffered a stroke. Vicky said that she had a pain in her neck behind her ear I asked if they could take the pain away. I asked spirit if they had something wrong with their neck. We caught an EVP saying 'Ethel'. I asked if they could tell us what happened to their neck and there was a big bang that came from the back room. I asked if they could do it again. I asked if they had a accident. Shayna wondered if they had done it on the stairs.

I asked if they had a fall and caught an EVP saying 'yes'. I could hear movement coming from the kitchen and asked if they would walk past the sensor on the floor and make it go off. We caught an EVP of a child saying 'no way'. I started to get a pain in my neck and Vicky said hers had gone. We had it in the same place. We caught an EVP saying 'I've took it off'. This seemed to confirm that spirit do put feelings on you to show what they had experienced.

I asked what had happened to their neck and asked if they had taken their own life and there was 3 taps on the microphone attached to the voice recorder. I said that they maybe didn't but it felt like a bit of a knot behind my ear. It then suddenly dawned on me that it could be Mrs Cotton and asked if it was her. There was a whistle caught on voice recorder. There was a tap in the room. I said that if it was her she doesn't usually communicate that easily.

I asked Mrs Cotton if she was with us and we all felt ice cold draughts around us. We caught a ladies voice on voice recorder saying 'Mrs Cotton couldn't go'. I asked if she had come to talk to us tonight and we caught an EVP saying 'Cotton'.

 I took out the thermal imaging camera to see if I could pick up the cold spots on camera and caught what looked like a child looking through the door. I told her that we didn't mean her any harm and that she should already know that. I said that maybe it wasn't Mrs Cotton and asked if it was anyone else. I asked them to tap on something if they were a man but didn't get a response. I asked if it was a lady but still no response.

Hannah was talking about a girl called Molly that she had picked up earlier. She said that she had brought someone with her but they were standing back. Molly was 13 and had brought someone younger. Shayna wondered if she had had an accident and hung accidentally. Hannah was shown Molly playing with a metal hoop and was wearing a long petticoat on, bloomers and boots. We caught a child groaning on Handy Cam. I asked if she was from the area or the shop. Hannah felt the area and she had now brought a man with her. She too had neck pain but it was different to mine. Hannah could also hear pit boots on the cobbles. I said that I had caught something on the thermal imaging camera and it was looking in the door from the outside. It was child height.

I thanked spirit for the evidence and said that it was lovely. Hannah was now picking up on a lady, quite stern like a school teacher. She walked with a limp and had problems with her left side. She got the name Grace and wore a long black dress. She felt that she was old but not very elderly. I said that they looked old.

I asked Grace if she had a stroke and we caught an EVP saying 'Grace'. Hannah said that all the kids in the area were scared of her. I asked her to tap on something if she did have a stroke or could she knock over the doll that was on the floor.

Hannah said Molly was dressed very similar to the dolls but her dress wasn't patterned it was a plain black dress. I felt that she had a stomach problem and Hannah said that she felt sickly with her but didn't know if she was scared of someone or had a problem with the stomach. I said that we had come to learn about her.

I noticed that the pendulums on the stand were moving and that no one was touching the table. I asked if they could touch them and if they wanted to communicate with them. Vicky felt that there was a draught passing by her towards them. I said that I could still see the energy swirling around in the room.

Hannah said that it was people coming and going and I said that we should do an EVP session. Then we caught an EVP on Handy Cam saying 'yes'. As I was getting the voice recorder Hannah was talking about an oldish man who used to come in the shop and used to give out boiled sweets.

Debbie said that it could be anyone as lots of older people have come and gone and because the shop has been closed due to the pandemic she didn't know if they were now in spirit. She said that there was a man used to offer sweets but she wasn't sure if he was in spirit.

I tried an EVP session.

Have you got some black bullets? I like a black bullet. Is there anyone here that passed with a stroke? We caught an EVP of a child saying 'yeah'. Did you have a stroke condition? Because I keep feeling like I have a mouth that has dropped. Can you give me your name please? Just come and talk to us a little bit. 'I'm going to put you in a book and tell the world about you. Shayna got the name George and I said the pain in my neck had come back.

Who's the person who has a problem with their neck? Can you tell me that bit? Were you hung? I know you won't want to talk about it. Hannah asked if it was male or female.

Are there any spirits with us can you come and talk to us please? Can you talk into this microphone please. Are you the gentleman that used to give away boiled sweets? I could do with a sweet. I don't mind if they have been in your pocket a month. Is Molly here? At that point I was seeing spirit lights in the room near Vicky. Who's the person who was stood in the doorway?

Hannah said that she had seen a little girl in the building opposite and she was waving at her. I said that she should wave back. We caught an breath on the voice recorder. Why don't you come down and talk to us? I said that it might have been the girl who was looking through the door.

Bev said that I should ask if his name was Bruce. We caught an EVP saying 'name'. she said that her dads friend passed to spirit and would come in the shop along with going up to Gregory's. She said that he always had boiled sweets in his pocket. Again we caught a breath on voice recorder.

Is this Bruce? Are you just popping in? Bev said he had brain cancer and passed with it. I said it was very sad. I said that they should try table tipping.

Vicky and Debbie tried table tipping but there wasn't any movement with the table. I did feel a person was stood to my right and was watching but maybe they felt that this wouldn't be suitable. We closed the session down and I turned on the portal.

Alright (man)

It's me (lady)

Molly (child)

Are you the little girl from over the road?

Yes (lady)

Hi.

Can you give us your name?

Yes (lady)

I went over to the shelf to pick up the Handy Cam.

Go back (man)

Is Molly here?

Cilla stuck (lady)

Did that say Cilla?

Shayna said that it may be their mum. I said that she's not in the spirit world but she thought that it could be a message for her mum.

Are these settings right?

Yes (lady)

Gregg (man)

I changed them and asked if they were right.

Yeah (man)

We can't hear you very clearly because we are too close.

Outside (man)

Are there any Greggs here?

Peter, Paula (man)

I thought it said Paula

Couldn't catch him. You're telling me (man)

The portal moved on its own but unfortunately I didn't catch it on camera. If I had left the Handy Cam where it was we would have. And the portal did say go back and this might have been why.

I asked if they could do it again.

No (man)

Everyone saw the wire move except me.

Derrick wright (man)

Did you say Paula?

Paula (man)

You said Grace before didn't you Hannah?

Liver (man)

Liver? Are you a butcher?

Yeah (man)

I don't like liver. Have you got any bacon?

My husband loves liver. He doesn't get it though.

Doesn't me? (lady)

Hannah said that David loves it and she doesn't cook it either.

No (man)

Love liver (man)

So, can you give me your first name please?

Bill (man)

I thought it said Bob. But said it would be easier to hear later on the recordings.

So, your Mr Gregg and you're a butcher? Can you tell us what year you were here?

It did reply but I couldn't hear it.

Hannah thought it said 26.

Did you say 26?

That'll be lucky (man)

Yes (man)

Out (man)

Do you just keep an eye on things?

We caught an EVP of a lady saying 'very'.

Yes (man)

Are you helping out?

Justine (man)

Wayne (or) win (lady)

Yes sir (lady)

Did you have a slaughter house here?

Shop (man)

Yes (man)

Where though? Out the back?

Hannah felt that there was an accident in the shop. And I asked what type of accident.

Yes (lady)

Hannah felt that somebody had badly cut themselves with a large knife.

Yes (man)

Did you cut yourself with one of those big knives?

Debra (man)

Can you tell me something about this building that no one knows and I've got to look for?

We caught an EVP on Handy Cam saying 'your birthday'.

John (man)

I thought it said back shop.

Was it rough around here?

Yes without dinner (man)

Yes (man)

Yes (lady)

Were there lots of prostitutes and brothels? I bet people used to tick on.

Yes (man)

Debbie and Shayna were talking about a brothel being closed close by not too long ago.

Death right there (man)

Yes (man)

I joked and said that I now knew why my husband liked to come to Bishop on a Friday night.

Yes (man)

Did people used to come and try to tick on?

Desperate (man)

Did (lady)

Did somebody rip you off? Because I keep getting theft.

Check (man)

Cheque? Did somebody give you a dodgy cheque? Did they have cheques?

Hannah and Shayna felt it was for me to check.

Guess what ian (man)

For me to check?

Yes (child)

Did it go to court? Or do I have to check that too?

Yes (man)

Hannah felt that something shady had gone on. I told the group that I kept being shown the police in my mind's eye.

Ben (lady)

Yes (man)

Did somebody did you wrong? Because I felt that you were a nice kind person.

Death (man)

Are you the one that's got a bad left leg?

Severed (man)

Bridget (man)

I said that I felt a problem with the leg and this person would walk with a stick.

Was it a war wound?

Yes (man)

Hannah felt shrapnel.

We caught an EVP saying 'the 2nd one'. Where they confirming it was shrapnel?

Are you on any of these photos?

Seven (man)

Who's the person with a bad neck, apart from me?

Bad pain (man)

Yes (lady)

Are you a lady? Did you have a bad neck?

Yes (man)

You didn't sound like a lady.

Great reply (man)

Why was I shown a rainbow this morning? Can you tell me that?

Shayna felt that It might have something to do with pride month. We talked about homosexuality years ago and that it was illegal.

Were you gay?

No (man)

I said that last time I asked they thought gay meant happy.

Were you homosexual.

No! (man)

I don't mean to upset you, I was just asking.

Help (man)

We then talked about an investigation that were on years ago and a man had come through to us. It wasn't very far from the shop but we cant mention it as it was a private investigation. This man had took his own life by hanging because he was homosexual. I wondered if this was the same man.

Yeah (man)

Come and tell us something about you and take this pain from my neck.

Tell me something amazing.

Did you work here, or live here?

Did here (man)

What year was it?

Who is the man with the black bullets?

Bob (man)

Black bullets (man)

Black bullets. Did you hear that? I'm sure it said black bullets.

Were they your black bullets? I like black bullets.

Boys (lady)

Boy?

The back steps (lady)

The back steps? How many spirits are in the room with us now?

Are there any back steps? Debbie said there aren't.

Let (man)

Did you used to have back steps?

Black bullets (man)

Maybe it was where they used to slaughter.

Are you waiting for us anywhere? Should we move through the back?

Sit (man)

Who is the girl who was waving from over the other side?

Annabelle (man)

Hello (man)

 I thought it kept saying Paula.

Yes (lady)

Who is Paula?

Are you wanting to get a message to Paula?

Paula (lady)

Please (lady)

You will have to give us a clue because I don't know who Paula is.

Yes (man)

Paula? What's Paula's second name?

Dunn (man)

Dunn? I asked Debbie if she knows a Paula Dunn but she didn't.

I will try and find a Paula Dunn. Maybe she will read the book as its happened before where people recognise people described.

True (man)

Don't do that to her (man)

I said that you could still see the energy in the room swirling.

It has a nice feeling in here though doesn't it?

Do you play tricks?

Bad tricks (man)

Do you touch people? Do you tap them on the shoulder? Do you think it's funny?

Here (man)

Yes (man)

Its lovely to talk to you. We have to go soon. We can't stay here all night.

Why? (man)

We are (man)

Come and tell me something gruesome and juicy.

Suspects (man)

It doesn't have to be about in here. Tell us something gruesome. Was there murder outside?

Bus (lady)

Who was arrested? Come and name them all.

Jean Gregg (man)

Debbie thought it said Jean Gregg

Come and tell us.

June (lady)

There's another dead fly.

Dead fly (man)

In the shop (man)

Did that say dead fly? (Bev)

Are you out the back?

Wait for us (man)

Should we come through there and see if we can sense you through there?

Im going to knock you off now. thanks for talking.

Ok (man)

Where the dogs are (man)

The portal started to make a loud noise and I said I was going to blow myself up.

A man laughed through the portal. I said he wasn't supposed to laugh at that. We said our thanks and turned it off. I said that he was very pleasant.

We moved to the back room and I asked the group if anyone was sensing anything. I felt that I had fallen and had a pain above my eye. I said that they had gotten us all in the room near the back step. I asked they had fallen in the room. Debbie said that the building next door was the butchers shop and the building we were in was the cottage. They had sold the shop and turned the downstairs of the cottage into a shop and lived upstairs.

I wondered where they would have a slaughter house. Vicky said that there was large wooden fridge in the room we were in. Debbie said there was a passage outside. We thought that maybe they just slaughtered one animal at a time.

Bev commented on how cold it was in the room. I said that it was cold beneath my knee and Hannah said it was around her legs. Debbie and Bev were talking about butchers and we talked about Debbie having a small holding with Wayne and having sheep and was a hobby. All the animals that are hand reared they keep them and the rest get sold.

I did an EVP session.

I asked if there was a child in the room and if they were around my legs. But I said that it could be an animal and they wouldn't answer.

We have to go soon, have you got something to say? Have you got a bad tummy? I said that I had that earlier in the evening and felt it was linked with the child.

What's wrong with your tummy? Maybe it's what you passed to spirit with? I wondered if it was linked to poisoning. Are there any children here related to Mrs cotton. I was wondered if that was why I was getting a watery mouth. We caught an EVP on the Handy Cam of a groan.

Isabella are you here? At that point Shayna felt a cold draught. You like to come and talk to us usually don't you. Did you come down the town? Maybe you came in here? I can't see your mam treating you to pork sandwiches to be fair. But maybe you did and you came in. Did you buy meat from here or maybe the butcher gave you some scraps. We played the voice recorder back and there was some taps on the recording. There was an EVP on Handy Cam saying 'get in'.

I said that there was a weird tapping on the recording.

Are you tapping on the microphone? Can you tap again? There was a tap on the Handy Cam.

Bev said that they may have come in to buy rabbits. I know you used to go to a butchers in West Auckland but Mrs Cotton liked to drink in the Sun Inn up the road. Is that right? Were you left in the house? I know we have spoken to you before and I know it's hard to talk about. Hannah said that they believed Mrs Cotton used to buy the arsenic in a chemist down the road from here and I didn't know that. I thought it was at West Auckland. Shayna said that she wouldn't buy it on her doorstep.

Did she used to come to a chemist here? We caught an EVP on Handy Cam saying 'no'.

I know that she was arrested and taken to the police station here and that she used to drink at the Sun Inn. Was that right? Shayna asked about the Sun Inn and I said that it is now at beamish. She asked where it used to be and it was very close to where we were. I asked if that was the right story. We played the recording back. The weird thing is that both Bev and Hannah's voices changed and sounded like elderly people.

Vicky started to have a weird sensation with her hands. I asked if the spirit had a problem with their hands and could they take the feeling away. I asked what they had wrong with their hands and what they were trying to tell us. I asked them to step back. I asked Vicky if it was still there. It was but it was right up the hands but was now just two fingers on both hands. I asked if they had their fingers wrapped as a punishment or did they get them trapped. I asked if they lost a finger. But both Hannah and I felt that it was the cane. We played it back and we had caught a moan on the recordings.

We made our way back to the shop and we asked if we could pop upstairs for a look. Debbie stayed downstairs but Vicky took us up. we talked about how lovely the shop is and how comfortable I felt in it. The stairs were very narrow and steep leading upstairs and I said I wouldn't like to climb them after drinking alcohol.

It was huge upstairs and I could feel energy in the room. I felt that someone had a problem had a problem with their chest. Shayna wondered if it would be emphysema. I felt that it was like pleurisy and went right through my chest to my back. I felt someone step really close to me and asked if they suffered with their chest. I felt that they struggled to breathe.

I asked if they smoked. Shayna asked if it was angina but I said I was struggling to breathe in. Hannah wondered if it was black lung. Shayna said that when you have angina you struggle to breathe.

I said it was really uncomfortable and I went really cold. I asked if it was Shayna's dad Colin as he had angina. I had been recording on the voice recorder and played it back.

Hannah asked Vicky if they heard walking in certain times of the day. Vicky confirmed that they often hear footsteps. I went for a look at the other rooms and felt that someone was following me around.

I asked Hannah if she was picking anything else up. she was picking up the strong energy of a man different to downstairs. She said that she could feel a vibration through her feet on the floorboards and asked me to stand there. I could feel a vibration right up my legs but Debbie couldn't feel it. I couldn't work out why it would be vibrating.

Hannah said that she went dizzy and could see the room the way it was. She said that there was once a coal fire somewhere as she could smell the smoke. But she felt very tired. This man was wearing a grandad shirt with a black suit. He had grey hair and he was so tired. There had been a family upset and fighting in the family somewhere and told me to watch for it. He felt tired and drained and was very poorly. He looked old but was about in his 50's but looked old for his time.

She wasn't sure if he was a pitman at some point and died young with his chest. I said that it was a very hard life and that they started work very young.

I said that we had to go and that it was lovely talking to him. Hannah felt he was Methodist and that this man went to a church nearby. I asked if there was difference with Wesleyan and Methodist as I thought Wesleyan. Hannah talked about Mary Ann Cotton again and the chemist was close. Debbie felt that Labyrinth used to be a chemist but she wasn't sure if she was imagining it. Hannah felt that Vicky was gifted and should learn to communicate with spirit.

We ended the investigation there. It had been a fascinating night and Vicky was really pleased that she had been given her own personal experiences. She comes along to our investigations and joined us at the Welcome Inn that is also featured in the book.

RESEARCH

A large house, pleasantly situated in Bondgate with ten fire rooms, with good garrets, cellars, brew-house, stable, pump, with a large garden, well planted with wall trees, and laid out pleasant walks with a grass garth, containing about 2 ½ acres, extending from the garden to the river wear advertised in a newspaper. It was in occupation of John Jepson, collector of excise. Also to be let, a good sized house, in Newgate, wherein a woollen-manufactory was carried by Mr Durant, deceased. The owner was Mrs Clark. This was in July 1738. The portal said John.

In May 1740, John Dunn, a merchant from Bishop Auckland died and his estate was up for sale. The portal said John, it also said Dunn.

There was an advertisement in a newspaper to be sold either together or separate, four closes on the south side of the river garnless, nigh Bishop Auckland, then in the possession of Percival Whitefield and others. And also the tithes of Bondgate in Auckland, Middridge and Coundon, all in the parish of St Andrew Auckland; with pollards hall in Bishop Auckland, and a large orchard, malting, and malt-kiln, and two burrough houses, with an orchard in Newgate, and a barn in Bondgate. Enquire of Edward Goddard in Durham or Mr William Apedaile in Bishop Auckland. This was in October 1749. The portal said Bill.

The Shepherd's Inn was built in the early 18th Century as a private residence by Dr Martin Dunn, apothecary. His wife was called Elizabeth. Elizabeth was brother of George Wensley of Darlington. The portal said Dunn.

There was an auction for a Dwelling house and public bakehouse in Back Bondgate, occupied by Ann turner and a freehold massuage, then used a butchers shop in Fore Bondgate, occupied by Mr William Fell, butcher. This was in March 1824. The portal said Bill.

An auction was held at the Assembly Rooms and one of the properties was an inn at Fore Bondgate and comprising an Assembly Rooms. It had a large garden with fruit trees, a saw mill, wood sheds and shops. It was occupied by William Proud. The portal said Bill.

A dwelling house, situated in Back Bondgate, went up for sale or let in July 1849. It was in occupation by Mr Benjamin Heighington, potter merchant. The portal said Ben.

In the 1851 census, James Gregg, was a China Dealer and lived at High Bondgate with wife Elizabeth, son James, son William, Son Robert, daughter, Hannah, son James, son Henry, servant Elizabeth Bradwell. Also living at the address was Robert Gregg, William Harrison, James Harrison and Ann Harrison. The portal said Bob and Bill.

In February 1853, John Moor, of Fore Bondgate, had an interim Order for Protection from Process granted.

In January 1854, an inquest was held in the boardroom at the workhouse on the body of Margaret Ann Thomson who was aged 11 months old. Isabella Wood, her mother, was charged with the murder. It was believed that Isabella had struck the child's head on the mantelpiece. The portal kept said an Isabella.

In August 1854 Mr John Camidge, (son of Dr Camidge of York) organist to the Bishop of Durham, afforded a great musical treat in the Assembly Rooms, Bishop Auckland.

Barbara Wright lived at Back Bondgate in October 1857. She was a widow and a charwoman. The portal said Derrick Wright. Could they be related?

There was a house and shop to let at the entrance of Fore Bondgate from the market place in December 1858. It was occupied by Mr Robert Hall a grocer. The portal said Bob.

In 1858, there was a post office in Fore Bondgate. Mr A Bainbridge was appointed the responsible duties of postmaster. At this time they were considering placing pillar letter-boxes around the town.

In September 1858, John Hulme, High Bondgate, made an application for a spirit licence. Mr Stephenson appeared on behalf of the Stockton and Darlington Railway to oppose the application as the didn't want a public-house being licensed in the vicinity of the railway. The portal said John and Shayna picked up on a George.

In 1860, William Gregg was charged for obstructing a footpath. They had different articles connected with their business on the path of Newgate Street. The portal said Bill.

In March 1860, John Wouldhalve, a mason from the town, was charged with stealing a fowl, the property of Mr. W. Smith (a game and poultry dealer) in Fore Bondgate. The prisoner was drunk at the time but denied the charge. He had a previous felony and was sent to the house of correction.

In November 1860, Isabella Gregg married Isaac Watson at St Ann's Church.

Ralph Gregg was born in 1863. Hannah (his sister) was born in 1865, Christiana (his sister) was born in 1868, and brother Robert (his brother) was born in 1869. His parents were James Gregg born 1809 and Eliza M. Thurman born 1809. Robert was born 1841, Hannah was born 1843, John Gregg was born 1846, Henry Gregg was born in 1849. James Greggs parents were Jon Gregg and Frances Spilman. James was a Glass and China dealer.

In July 1867, Adam Harrison, alias Tap Harrison, a pitman belonging West Auckland, struck John Allen several times killing him. John Allen was a shoemaker, and lived at South Church. His body was found on the highway near Railway Terrace Forge. The body was moved to the Sun Inn, at Blue Row. The Portal said John.

In 1868, a fatal accident occurred to a little girl, about two years of age, named Elizabeth Alton, whose parents lived at Bondgate. The child was toddling across the street, and without being noticed by the driver of a cart in the employ of Mr H. Boardman, was knocked down and run over causing such injuries across the chest as to cause death within 15 minutes of the accident.

In July 1869, George Bradford was indicted for having robbed James Connor, with violence at Bishop Auckland. Shayna picked up on a George.

Mary Ann cotton was up on remand at the police court, charged with the poisoning of her stepson Charles Cotton aged 10 years and her own son Robert Robson Cotton aged 14 months old. This was in 1873. Was this Bob that came through on the portal? I asked if Mrs Cotton was with us and we received responses. We also caught EVP's saying 'Mrs Cotton couldn't go'.

James Batey and John Kipling were arrested and charged for playing at pitch and toss at the corner of George Street. This was featured in 1873. The portal said John.

In July 1879, George Alderson, a second-hand clothes dealer, Fore Bondgate, was fined £1 and costs for assaulting Henry Johnson, fish hawker, Newton Cap Bank by striking him in the eye. Shayna picked on George.

There was a cabinet maker called John Murray who lived on George street, I know that this building was featured in a newspaper article in 1879 and it seems like he went bankrupt in 1899. The portal said John.

In the 1881, census Frank Albion Bainbridge, a butcher, lived at 46 Fore Bondgate with wife Mary Ann Bainbridge, daughter Ethel, and son William Francis Bainbridge. Isaac Hodgson, a boot and shoe manufacturer lived at 47 Fore Bondgate with wife Mary Ann, and daughters Elizabeth, Charlotte and Sarah Jane. The portal said Bill and we caught an EVP saying 'Ethel'.

In the 1881 census, George and Jane Elsbury Charles lived at 14 Finkle Street with son Charles who was a widower and granddaughter Margaret. Shayna got the name George.

In the 1881 census, Jane Wiglet lived at 22 Fore Bondgate and was a Temperance hotel keeper. Is this why I was picking up the Temperance church.

In the 1881 census, William Smith was a butcher and game dealer at 3 Fore Bondgate. His wife was called Emily, son Wilfred, Susannah Braithwaite was a visitor and Sarah Brown was a servant. The portal said Bill.

In May 1881, Walter Tobin, an ironworker of middle age was locked up by Inspector Mutimer on a charge of wounding George Percival, Clayton Street by biting off his ear. The police couldn't find the missing ear. Shayna picked up on the name George.

In March 1882, a man named George Wilks, better known as 'Rag George' a native of Staffordshire and whose wife was in gaol, died in "little tenters" Bishop Auckland. He died penniless and friendless, and the relieving officer had to apply for a coffin and hearse, which did arrive but there wasn't anyone there to place the body in the coffin. Mrs Garfield, the wife of a pensioner, living in the same place, succeeded with the help of her husband. They had to screw down the lid, put it in the hearse, and remove the coffin at South Church. They called via the workhouse and hoped some inmates would help but they were unsuccessful. They were helped by 2 men working on a colliery cart who help get the coffin to the church but they didn't have anyone to help get it to the graveside. They obtained a sexton and managed to get it to his final resting place.

In march 1886, James Munroe from Glasgow was brought up in custody over passing a counterfeit half-crown to James Gregg, Pork butcher at Bishop Auckland. I kept picking up on a theft and someone getting ripped off at the shop.

In March 1886, Mr James Gregg, the oldest tradesman in Bishop Auckland died at the age of 79 years. Some of his sons carried on the business.

A Six ton memorial, made in America and shipped to Bishop Auckland was erected in the towns cemetery in 1890. It was to honour Robert Watson, born in Hamsterley in 1819, he started as a farmhand but ended up mayor of Lee's Summit, a city near Kansas City in the United States. Robert was an inspector on the Stockton and Darlington Railway and then on the London & North Western Railway. He then moved to a similar post on the newly-built Chicago & Alton Railroad, which ran through the US state of Illinios to Kansas City. The portal said Bob.

In the 1891 census, William Gregg was a china dealer, he lived with wife Jane, son Ralph, a butcher, daughter Hannah, son Robert, a butcher, daughter Mary Pallister, son in law, John Walker Pallister, Granddaughter Lizzie, and grandson Richard at Victoria House. The portal said John, Bob and Bill.

In the 1891 census, James Gregg, pork butcher, lived at 10 Grey Street with wife Jessie, Daughter Jennie and servant Ruth H Daykin.

In February 1891 at Clayton Street, Mr William Castling, a postman, died aged 38 years. The portal said Bill.

Robert O'Neill, aged 12, of Back Bondgate was arrested in April 1894 on a charge of causing the death of William Wilson, aged 13, of South Church by striking him on the head with a stick in the market place. The deceased boy's father was called George Wilson. The portal said Bob and Bill.

In April 1894, William Wilson, died after being assaulted. The deceased was an errand boy of Mr Cherrett, who was on the sick at the confectionery stall kept by W. H. Smith, of Spennymoor, in Auckland Market. H O'Neil, 12, the accused boy was at the inquest. William Eyeington, 12, Finkle-street said he and the other boys were about the stall. He said the accused struck the boy and he put his hand up to his head. William Coglan, 13, Wilkinsons-yard said he and the others were teasing him. The accused said he had been hit on the eye, then he got a stick, struck deceased with it, went away, returned and struck him again on the head. Willie Dodds, 13, back Bondgate heard the accused say that he would hit the deceased because the latter had struck him in the eye. Lionel Kipling, fish stall keeper, saw the deceased receive one blow from behind, but he couldn't identify the assailant. John Irwin, 12, Bondgate, said the accused had a mark on his eye. G. W. Smith said the boys kept striking the deceased as they passed the stall end. They did so because the boy was quiet; the regular boy wouldn't have endured that sort of thing. The accused was charged with manslaughter. The portal said Bill.

In 1894, Robert Gregg, a butcher from Bishop Auckland, was fined 10s 6d for drunkenness.

Donald Smart, aged 17, a French polisher who formerly lived in Huddersfield was charged with maliciously wounding an elderly man called John Lowe of Finkle street with a knife. This was is October 1894. The portal said John.

In May 1896, a bazaar was opened at the Bishop Auckland Temperance Hall. Miss Gregg, along with many others were in charge of sales. Is this why I was picking up the Temperance Church?

In November 1896, John Peart, aged 32, watchman and checker at the Auckland goods shed, was run over and killed by a heavily laden passenger brake going to West Auckland. The portal said John.

In 1899, Ralph Gregg was a bearer at the funeral of Mr Jno. Chas. Gregory. They carried Jacks coffin because they were in the same business as him.

In august 1899, there was a collision between a cyclist and a butchers cart, which occurred on Tenters Street. Geo. Robinson sued Robert Gregg, pork butcher for damage to his bicycle. Mr Gregg had to pay for damages. The portal said Bob.

In the 1901 census, Ralph Gregg, a butcher lived at 11 Tenters Street with wife Mary, mother Jane, and sister Christiana, daughter Essie, son John, Ada Parkin, a bread maker and general servant Mary Barrass. The portal said John.

In the 1901 census, Jane Gregg lived at 1 Low Waldron Street with Grandsons Frederick (a postman), George (a Grocers assistant) , and granddaughter Sylvia.

There was a lady called Mary Hewitt residing in George Street that was knocked down by a bus, this was featured in the newspapers 1900. Was this the bus that the portal mentioned?

In 1907, Frederick Gregg was a postman.

In January 1907, there was an accident at Newgate Street. Robert Dent was clearing snow when he slipped. A cart went over his left leg. Robert Dent lived at George Street. The portal said Bob.

In the 1911 census, Thomas Stubbs, a master house painter lived at 47 Fore Bondgate with wife Susannah and General Servant Margaret Wilson. There was a shop and 3 rooms.

In the 1911 register, Mrs Margaret Hart lived at 8 Fore Bondgate it was a house and shops.

In the 1911 census, John D Gregg, Railway Platelayer, Elizabeth A. Gregg, Sydney W. Gregg, hairdresser lived at 37 Fore Bondgate.

In the 1911 census, Ralph Gregg, a pork butcher lived at 11 Tenters Street with wife Mary, mother Jane, daughter Essie, sons John and Norman Raine, Niece Elizabeth Spence and servant Margretta Collighan.

In the 1911 census, Robert Gregg, aged 43, a hawker, lived at High Bondgate with wife Sarah Jane, aged 39, son Robert, aged 18, a pony driver, Jane, aged 13, William, aged 10, Henry, aged 9, Christiana, aged 7, Benjamin, aged 3. The portal said Bob and Bill.

Robert Gregg signed up for the Royal Engineers on 19th October 1914 the age of 22 years and 2 months. He was based at York. His father was W. Gregg residing at 99 Bondgate. He was arrested in 1915 for drunkenness and creating a disturbance in the camp, he was arrested again in 1916 for drunkenness and striking a superior officer and again 1917 for striking a comrade. His list of offences on his recorder include being late or absent, drunkenness even in the field, fighting and gambling. The portal said Bob.

In 1919, he was sent to London with the army and his leaving address was 19 fore Bondgate.

Robert married Ethel (surname unknown) in 1921 and they had 6 children. Doris, Marjorie, Sarah, Ronald, Margaret and Lilian. Robert died in 1938. Ethel married David William Bowen in 1901 and Walters sister was called Pricilla. The portal said Cilla, Bob and Bill. We also caught an EVP saying 'Ethel.'

In 1915, Sydney Walker Gregg from 37 Fore Bondgate signed up for service. His next of kin was Selina Gregg. Sydney was a hairdresser. He joined the Royal Fusiliers.

Miss Ethel Kay lived in Finkle Street in 1934. We caught an EVP saying 'Ethel'.

In the 1939, register Benjamin Gregg was a master butcher at 8 Fore Bondgate, he lived with wife Phyllis, daughter Norma, domestic Edith Raine, and Freda Coates who looked to have been a lodger. The portal said Bed.

In November 1952, a fire engine skidded on an icy road, crashed through a fence and overturned in a field between Shildon and Bishop Auckland. The driver, Robert Denham, aged 32, from Grainger Street was taken to hospital with injuries and shock. The portal said Bob.

In the 1911 census, there was a Robert Ballan who lived at 33 Market place with his parents Peter and James (this is what the records say), brother Joseph and son Robert. The portal said Peter and Bob. We also picked up a Peter on a previous investigation at the Snooker Club which is close by.

The portal said Wayne, who is related to Debbie. It also said Debra.

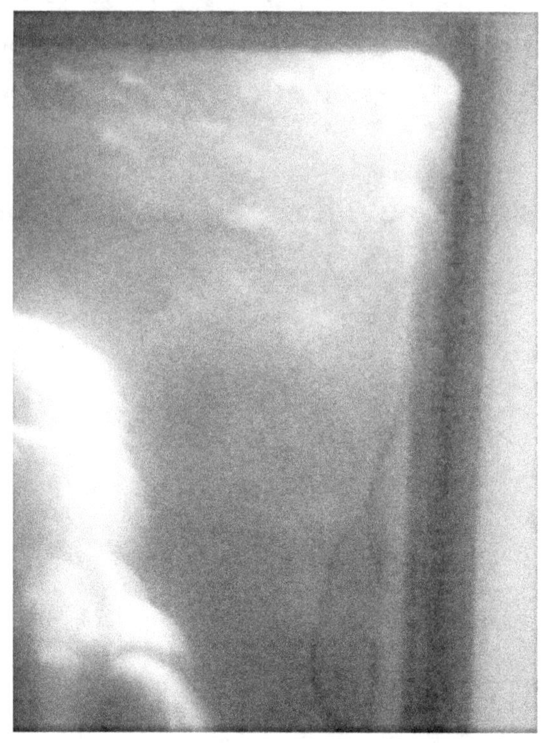

UPSTAIRS

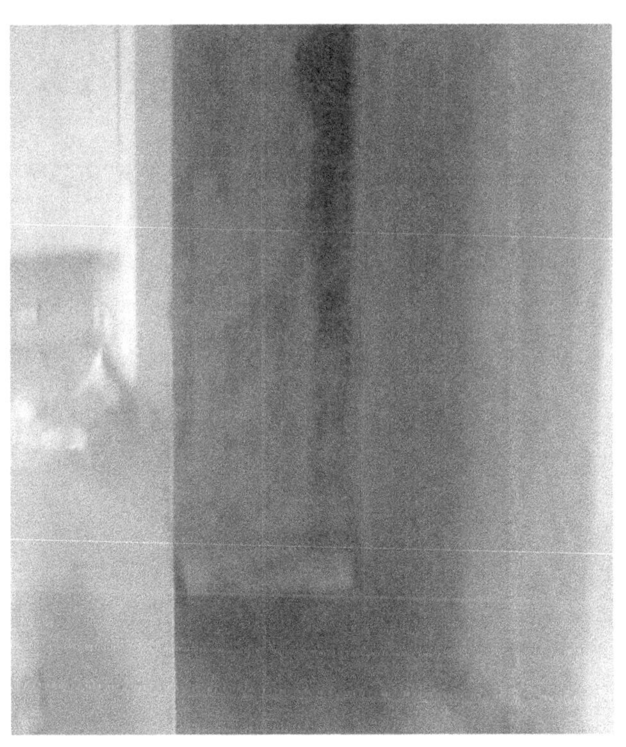

BEING WATCHED FROM UPSTAIRS

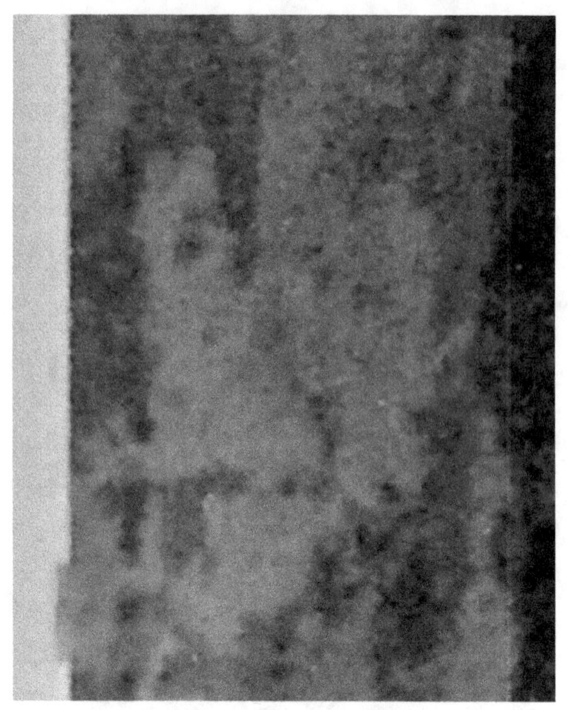

FIGURES UPSTAIRS

DOWNSTAIRS

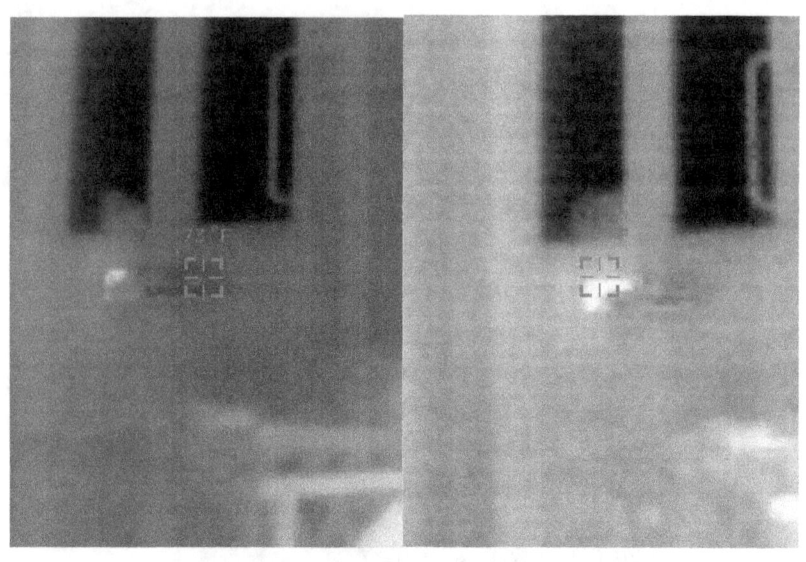

A CHILD LOOKING THROUGH THE DOOR CAUGHT ON

THERMAL IMAGING CAMERA

LABYRINTH

I noticed an article that had been featured in the local press about a radio presenter doing a quick investigation at Labyrinth and he stated that he felt a spirit at the premises that was linked to Mary Ann Cotton.

Given our history with Mrs Cotton, I contacted Diane and Angie and asked if we could investigate the shop in the hope of featuring it in our next Bishop Auckland book. They said yes immediately and we arranged the date for July 2021.

A couple of weeks before we had investigated Gregg Bros in the same street and had some amazing results.

When we arrived Diane and Angie were sat waiting eagerly for us. I knew that the shop was full of lovely things and there wasn't much room and was quite worried that we would knock something off the shelves but Diane assured us that all breakages were insured but that didn't make me feel any less uneasy!

You could feel an energy as soon as you walked into the shop and when we went through to the back you could feel the change in atmosphere. I picked up on a person who had a bad shoulder and felt sickness. Hannah was aware of a male energy. Bev and Shayna were too attracted to the shiny things on display to notice.

I set off the Handy Cam and voice recorder. I went through the back to place the REM pod on the floor and we placed the doll on a table that had a ring of ivy on it. We said the prayer and started the investigation.

Shayna started to feel sick and I had felt sick earlier but didn't now. Hannah asked Angie and Diane and if you could feel that the shop was lovely one minute and that the atmosphere changed immediately and they confirmed it. She said one minute it felt lovely and the next like something was going to happen and felt on edge. I said that suddenly I felt icy cold and Shayna said that something had just touched her on the back.

I felt that someone had just stepped into my aura and you could feel the coldness in the room. I invited the ladies to feel the coldness next to me. Because of the height of the coldness I felt that it was a child. Shayna said that she felt stomach pain and felt sick and wondered if it was a poison.

The ladies felt the cold and could feel the cold on top of their hand. I felt that it was a child. I could even work out by the energy that it was a child's height. I felt that it was a girl and she was very cold. I felt that I knew who it was and that we had met before. Diane said that she was now shivering.

I asked if it was Isabella and Bev felt that something pricked her leg. I asked her to walk through the back room and make the REM pod go off. I said that it was all pretty colours. I said that she will love all of the pretty things and would be having a great time behind closed doors. Isabella Mowbray was Mary Ann Cottons daughter who died at the age of 8.

I asked if she wanted to play with the doll. I moved the case as it was blocking her way. I also felt things around my legs and wondered if it was Isabella's cat. I asked anyone else if they could sense her and Hannah felt a little girl. She also felt a man and that he was the one that changed the atmosphere. Shayna said that someone touched her head.

I asked Hannah if she knew who he was and she said that it was way back. Shayna got the name Bob. I asked if he was in the back room. She said that that was his safe place but he did come out. She felt that he was in the shop before WW1 but did fight in the war and came home. He was in shell shock when he returned and was very nervous. He didn't harm anyone and she picked up the name Tommy but didn't feel it was his name but he was talking about Thomas. His injuries were mainly in his head. She was also picking up on another man who worked there after that. He was wearing a white apron and a black shirt. He had a moustache and was showing himself when he was younger. He was very strict and people were scared of him. I asked if she knew what he did and she felt it was his shop. His shoes were very shiny and he was very well kept. He used to go to the barbers for a shave and kept that façade.

Shayna asked if there was a butchers around here and we said that we were there at Greggs and that the other butchers was at the Auckland Cupcake Company.

Hannah was still on with the man and she could smell that everything was clinical. I asked if he had a name but he wasn't giving it. I said it I asked out would he give it but we thought he wouldn't take instructions from a woman.

Shayna felt that someone had a bad leg and was a butcher called James. She wasn't sure if someone had lost a leg. I asked Bev to feel my back as it was freezing. Diane said that it was always cold in the shop. Was she picking up on James Gregg?

I asked Isabella if she could move the doll. Hannah was picking up the name Constance and said it was residual. I said Constance? That's a nice name. We caught an EVP of a lady whispering 'Constance' on Handy Cam. Bev asked if anything had come off the shelves or anything. Diane said that the whole of the top shelf out the back came down. It could have been very dangerous.

I asked Hannah if I should do some EVP's and the energy had now shifted so did an EVP session.

Isabella are you here with us? I can feel you around me and we don't mind that your here. It's nice to see you. Can you talk into the microphone and I'll be able to here you. Are you still cold? Some of the display moved behind me and I heard it move. On the voice recorder a little voice said 'help'. Isabella is that you? Did you brush past it?

Bev noticed that the artificial flowers were moving. Can you do that again that's a good game? They aren't breakable that's a good thing to touch. You don't need to be shy. I'm guessing that your mammies not here if you're here. When we played it back we could hear someone asking for help again.

Angie said that the hairs were standing up on the back of her neck after listening to the recording.

Isabella? Is you that is asking for help? What can we help you with? You have to tell us because we don't know. Are you lost? Have you lost your brothers and sisters? Come and give us an idea? If it isn't Isabella that needs help and can you tell us who does? We mean you know harm and we will help you if we can.

I'm not going to ask you anymore Isabella because I don't want to upset you. So if you have anything to say you just say it. If you want to move the plants you move them, if you want to punch Bev you punch her. I asked Hannah if there was anything happening at the bottom end of the shop and she said that there was movement in the back room. I asked the child to knock the doll off but to be careful where she knocked it towards. Hannah said the man was a bit touchy feely. I shouted that we were coming down and didn't mean him any harm. I said how lovely the smell was in the back shop and I was stood near to the shelf that fell. I moved out of the way as the shelf was really heavy and was scared it would happen again.

I asked who the person was who knocked the shelf down and were they playing tricks. Shayna was sniffing the wax pot as it smelled lovely. I felt it was really hot in the room but Hannah was freezing.

I asked Hannah if she was aware of the man and she said he loved it in there. Hannah asked the ladies if they had ever been touched on their back as he kept touching her on the back of her coat.

Shayna felt that she was touched when she was close to the door. She felt it was maybe a child because of the height.

I asked if we should do an EVP session in the room and we did. I asked Hannah if she had the man's name. I said that I had a bad shoulder again. She said he liked the bottles and I wondered if he was a chemist. When she looked and saw the bottles she knew that was why he liked it.

As I was recording Hannah said the man liked the room because of the brown coloured bottles that were on the shelf. As we were talking we caught an EVP of a man laughing.

Can I ask, the gentleman that's in this room with us now, were you a chemist? They weren't called chemists were they? I don't think they were called chemists. Pharmacist. Were you a pharmacist can you let me know please? Do you like the brown bottles? We caught an EVP saying 'definitely'. It's quite a nice area back here, it feels nice. And it smells nice. I bet that's why you like it. Did you knock the shelf down? I wouldn't like to think that came down on me, mind. Hannah said that it would take a lot of energy to knock it down.

Diane said the he used to be an Apothecary. That was the word that I couldn't think of. I knew it wasn't chemist and Diane said that it would make sense that he liked the brown bottles. Hannah said that he liked the shape and the glass stopper. Shayna wondered if Arsenic was in a brown bottle too.

Were you a op.....herbalist? I like herbs. Hannah said that she likes herbal tea and loved the cups in the shop. Is this why you are here? For these bottles? They are lovely mind, they are lovely bottles. Does it take you back to when you were a herbalist or a oppy poppy wappy poppy or whatever you were. Hannah was seeing a waxy substance like soap and he was putting powder in with it. I said it wasn't arsenic was it and was it bed bug soap that they used to clean the mattress with. It did sound like bed bug soap and said I would ask.

Did you make bed bug soap and did Mrs cotton buy it from here? Million dollar question! Did she buy it from here? Did she buy her arsenic from here? I started to get a slavery mouth again. Are any of the cotton children here? We caught a man on voice recorder saying 'one'. Isabella are you trying to tell us that this is where it was bought from? I know it's awful and a horrible subject but we'll never know if you don't tell us. You have to tell us. We heard a bottle clanking sound. I asked if they could do it again. Which one of these bottles did it look like? Which shape was it? Can you clink it? No? Are you not going to do it?

I asked Hannah if she had a name with the herbalist but she said he wouldn't give it. She said that he made candles too. Shayna got the name Wilfred and Diane thought that Wilfred came through on the other investigation. I said that there was a candle maker in fore Bondgate I'm sure there was. Diane said that she had suddenly got an awful taste in her mouth and I asked spirit to take it off. Hannah asked if it tasted metallically. I asked Isabella if it was her to step away and take the taste away. I said that I knew it was awful and that I was really surprised she had come if this was where they bought the arsenic from. I asked if she had just wanted to tell her story. Hannah heard a noise and I thought that I did too. I said that I had the slavery mouth. I said that we were going to go out and put the portal on and that she could tell us what she needed help with. I asked if Mr herbalist was coming with us and if he had a bad shoulder. I felt that it was arthritis.

We decided to make our way back into the main shop to carry on with the investigation. As we were walking back in we caught the EVP of a cat meowing on the Handy Cam. I know there was probably a cat at the shop as they controlled the mice but Isabella also wanted a cat when we investigated the home of Mrs Cotton many years before.

I thought it would be a good idea to turn the lights off in the back end and see if I could capture some photos. Hannah came with me as she didn't feel comfortable wIth me being in there alone with such a strong presence. Remember he could make a very heavy shelf come away from the wall!

As I joined the rest of the team on the shop we thought now would be a good time to do a portal session.

Shop, mine (man)

Alright (man)

Hello.

Jim (man)

Eric?

Careful (lady)

Careful? What am I being careful about?

Can you come and talk to me please?

Filling pots (man)

Yes (man)

Did you say your names Eric?

Get out (man)

Out? Do you not want us here?

Is Isabella here?

Yes (lady)

Was that a yes?

Isabella (man)

Isabella?

Yes (child)

What does Isabella need help with?

Philip (man)

Back (lady)

I'm trying to make it louder.

Who has to get back?

Jack, Kevin (lady)

I did (child)

Isabella I'm going to sit on the floor next to you. Alright?

I've brought a toy. (I started to play the kalimba) Are you going to play?

Yes (man)

Did Mrs cotton buy her arsenic here?

Yes (man)

No?

Yes (lady)

Soap?

The carrier bag started to move.

Floor (man)

Floor? Who's moving my bag?

The kids (man)

Horrors (or) Horace (man)

What are you looking for?

Can you lift it up?

Kids (or) Chisholm (man)

Peter (man)

Are you after something?

Give me five minutes (cockney man)

Are you after something?

Don't you want to play with this? It's much more exciting than a carrier bag.

Never (man)

Shayna asked if they would have had carrier bags back then and we said no.

Hannah felt that she was after food.

Do you think there's food in? I don't think there is? There's a can of pop in there.

I don't have any food.

Eat (man)

Are you hungry?

She cannot be (man)

Are you still cold and hungry?

The bag was still moving a lot.

Catherine (lady)

Go on, give it a good whack. Its lovely to see you.

If I had something to give you, I would give you it but I haven't.

Go (child)

Can you say your name?

Is it Isabella?

Yes (man)

Or is it one of the other children?

Eric (man)

That's twice it said Eric.

Who is Eric? Is it the herbalist?

Potts (man)

Frederick?

Problems (man)

Freddy (lady)

Frederick cotton?

Is it Frederick cotton? Did you get called Eric.

Blue (boy)

Are you here with Isabella?

Yeah I'm here (man)

Eric, here (man)

It's nice to hear from you if it is you.

I asked Hannah if she was picking anything up. she said that they were just watching. She also said that here were a couple of bangs.

You can see us (man)

Can you said something really clear for me?

Phyllis (lady)

Phillip? Who's Phillip?

The flats (man)

Who is Philip?

Should I change the channel?

Spectres (man)

Yeah (lady)

Bev asked if the settings where the same as Hexham but it had been in the box and will have altered. I changed the channel

Hannah was aware of a Peggy and asked what it was short for. We said Margaret.

Who is Peggy?

Is Peggy here?

Nothing came through the portal.

Shayna said the name John Jacobs.

Hannah said that we had had that name before and tried to remember where from.

I changed the channel back.

Put it back (man)

Freddy stops (man)

Can you say something really clear?

Here (man)

Been touched (man)

Can you tell me something about this building please?

Leave (man)

Was it a chemist?

Gregg bros (man)

Was it a herbalist? I keep saying chemist but you weren't were you.

Hi, ben (lady)

Who was moving my bag?

I'm going to go through the back.

Ok (man)

And I'm just going to shine it in the dark and if you want to be on this camcorder you can be.

I'm not coming in because I don't want to fall over things.

If you want to be can you be on this film, can I catch you.

(The portal was playing in the main shop and I was out the back but the camcorder did pick the words up).

Fred Allen (lady)

Desperado (man)

Come back (man)

Can you show yourself to me on this camera please?

Old fool (man)

The ladies were talking about an ironmongers.

Good afternoon (lady)

I don't know if I've caught you or not I can't see.

Hannah said for me to ask him to stand where the bottles are, she had following me.

Hannah was freezing. I kept seeing a face in front of the camera.

Where you showing yourself on my camera?

Ian (lady)

Its love to see you and its lovely to talk to you.

Something touched my arm. Hannah said that the presence was definitely with us.

Bob (man)

Did you have a problem with your arm?

I asked the ladies if it was doing their head in and should I knock it off?

Are you sick of us now?

Please sir (man)

Bev thought that it said 'Piss off'.

Hurry (lady)

Hurry? Are you sick of us?

Because he's here (man)

We don't want to outstay our welcome.

Should I knock it off?

Shayna said that John Jacobs was an ironmonger.

I'm going to knock you off, thanks for talking to me ok?

Thanks bitch (man)

Goodnight.

I knocked the portal off and asked Shayna about the iron monger. She also felt that Philip made coffins. I said I was still getting the slavery mouth and asked the ladies if they wanted to try table tipping and we caught an EVP saying 'help'.

We placed the table in the back room and Diane moved one of the stands to make room. I did the table with Angie and Diane and I made sure we were protected before we started. As soon as we placed our hands on the table it started to turn.

If there are any spirit in the room with us can you move this table please? Can you twist it for me?

Can you lift it? It started to move more. It seemed like it wanted to twist it.

Angie's hands had gone very purple. I started to say well done and it came out Willy. I asked who Willy was and Shayna said that she got Wilfred earlier. I asked if it was William or Wilfred.

I asked if they could turn it a little bit more. I asked if this was the man that Hannah was aware of and to turn it if it was but it didn't turn.

I asked if he worked there, did he own the building, did he live in the street. Was it a herbalist? Was he still here?

I asked who Eric was and it moved. I asked if Eric was the herbalist. I asked if Eric was Frederick. I asked if it was a Cotton and was any of the Cotton's were there.

Shayna felt sick.

I asked if there were any children there. I asked if there were any relations to the cotton there could they turn it fully. I could see it moving and asked them to twist it or lift it on two legs.

I asked if it was the man who made the shelf come down.

Was it Isabella? No.

Is it Mrs Cotton? No.

Is it Mr Cotton? No.

We were all starting to hurt.

We said purple. When we had investigated Hexham it said purple.

Did you know we were coming?

Diane left the table leaving Angie and I.

I asked Hannah if she knew who it was because I was lost. She said that I would find him.

I asked if it was John Jacobs, Tommy? I asked if he made coffins?

Hannah said that I would find him as he was the herbalist but he can't say who he is

I felt that the spirit had left the table.

I said that we were going to call it a day as my knees were hurting and asked to move it before we finished. It started to move again. Shayna had a cold spot on her head. I asked if they had something to say. I asked if they were happy the way things were run now. I asked if they loved the lovely smells and lovely things and did they play with it when the lights went out.

I asked if they moved things and hide things. I asked if they were weary of the man and did he run a tight ship. I asked if they would tip it to say goodnight. Shayna felt that something touched her arm.

We finished the session and thanked them. I said that they had done really well as it takes a lot of energy.

We made our way back into the shop to finish the investigation. Hannah was at the back of the shop with Angie and Diane talking to them about the spirits.

Diane asked Hannah if she picked things up in front of the jewellery display as loads of people said that they have felt something there. Hannah said she gets the shudders when she stands there and felt that it was connected with a lady. She said that people may have experienced being touched. She felt that the lady was building, it wasn't nasty but she would make her presence known. I asked if it was Peggy. She felt that this lady was attracted to the jewellery. I asked if she was getting anything else and she felt it was early 1900's. I said they wouldn't have had much jewellery. She felt that she had been wronged and something happened to her. I asked if she was light fingered but she said she wasn't. I was aware of a lady who was and she told me she would 'have them'. Hannah asked if things had gone missing and they said they had. I felt that the lady I had was a lady of the night. Hannah felt that this lady was a strong energy and people would pick up on it.

She felt that if anyone come in wearing nice things to watch out for them being touched. Hannah told them to tell them that it was there space and to tell them. I said that sometimes they try to get your attention and try too hard and you sometimes have to have a word with them to back off slightly. I said that the kids would have a field day in there and the lady of the night definitely fancies the goods.

Angie said that a lady comes in and says she sensed spirit in the shop. I said that you can see the energy in the shop, just like we did at Gregg bros. I thought there was that many layers coming and going and they all leave an impression and that when they know we are doing this they know it's their time to come and talk.

They were happy that the spirits were there and Hannah said there was a lot of energy all on different layers and it was like opening a history book. I said that we could come back a million times and get different things. Diane said that it would be interesting to see what we would pick out in the street.

We were talking about Stan Laurel and where he had come through and Angie had her elbow touched. Angie said that they had a teapot in tribute to Mrs Cotton and it was on the shelf and dropped off leaving a chip on the rim. I pointed out that Mrs Cotton's teapot that is in beamish has a chip in the rim so that was probably why. Angie said that she had been to Beamish to see the teapot.

We decided to call it a night as the energy had dropped and Hannah felt that they had said their piece. We called it a night and said the prayer.

I didn't know that the portal had said Fred Allen when I was in the back room. Fred Allen was my uncle. It also said Ian who was my godfather and my cousin husband.

RESEARCH

In the 1841 census, Nicholas Gregson was a joiner at Bondgate. He used to make coffins.

In October 1851, a mansion house in High Bondgate street went up for auction. It had Two drawing rooms, library, bed rooms and domestic office with a coach house, stables, cow byer and other requisite out buildings and a large walled garden, well stocked fruit trees, and containing half an acre of land, with a brick-built summer house, and a terraced walk, commanding an extensive and beautiful prospect of the valley of the wear. Also Two cottages adjoining the mansion, a paddock, and a field of rich grass land. It was in the occupancy of Thomas Peacock Esq. There was also Four dwelling houses, with a large yard and out-offices and a blacksmiths shoeing shop commonly called the New Stables. This lot formed the upper ends of Fore Bondgate Street and Back Bondgate Street, where they unite and form High Bondgate Street and has Three different fronts. Shayna picked up on a Thomas.

A freehold house and Shop situated in Fore Bondgate was put up for auction. It was occupied by Mr John Elwin, grocer. And Two cottages, in Back Bondgate were up for auction at the same time. They were occupied by William Graham, Margaret Wilson and others. This was in

November 1853. The portal said Jack, which is short for John. It also said Peggy which is short for Margaret.

In January 1854, an inquest was held at the Work house on the body of Margaret Ann Thompson, a child about a year old. it was suspected that her mother Isabella caused the death by striking her head again the fire place. She was charged with Wilful Murder. The portal said Peggy, which is short for Margaret and it said Isabella.

In March 1858, James Allason, of Wheatbottom, potter, was charged with leaving his horse and waggon in Fore Bondgate. The portal said Jim.

In September 1865, there was an inquest held at the police court. Catherine Cortilla was killed by blow to the head which was received by Pat McGowan at Powell's Yard. John Cortilla was Catherine's brother. The portal said Catherine. The portal also said John at Greggs Bros.

Elizabeth Robertson was charged by John Race, beerhouse-keeper, Finkle Street, with refusing to quit his beerhouse when ordered to do so. This was in 1868. The portal said Jack which is short for John.

In November 1872, James Cree was charged with cutting and wounding Ann McKenna at Finkle Street. The woman's daughter, who was 16, was at the defendants house which was a house of ill-fame and she went and asked for her. He said she wasn't there and she said she wouldn't leave without her daughter. He took a coal rake and struck her on the head. The house was used as a brothel.

In October 1875, a man of weak intellect named John Hall, alias 'daft Jack' was going along the market when some persons knocked his pipe out of his mouth, whereupon he seized a cheese knife off a stall and stabbed a fruiterer named Alexander Adams, of Easingwold, who was passing. The portal said Jack.

John Kilburn, James Jackson, and Julia brady lived in Finkle street and were featured in an article about a suspicious death in 1875. James Lannon and James Jackson went to Jacksons house at Finkle street and a man was laid down in his house and was bleeding from the back of head. Joseph Foster lodged with Jackson along with some women of low character. John Terry admitted to Joseph Foster that he was responsible. He said that he threw him down the stairs and jumped on his guts. The deceased was called Edward Wilkinson. The portal said John. We have also had evidence that links with this at the Snooker club on a previous investigation. The portal said Jim. The portal at Greggs Bros said John.

Margaret Campbell, Ellen Tobinson, Mary Farmer and Charlotte Burke, women of ill-fame, were brought up on remand before Mr J. Jobson charged with drugging and robbery. These ladies were listed as unfortunates, which is another name for prostitutes. This was in 1876. The portal said Peggy, which is short for Margaret and the

Talker 2 said Mary. I picked up on a prostitute who fancied the goods. Was this one of these ladies?

There was a theft in Finkle Street, Ralph Ridley had money stolen by Mary Campbell, Ellen Robinson, Mary Farmer and Charlotte Bourke (Four ladies of disreputable character) and Charles Johnson in 1876. The Talker 2 said Mary.

Fred Ward was taken to court charged with assaulting Ellen Williams, a disreputable character, living in Finkle Street. This was in October 1876. The portal said Fred.

In August 1876, Margaret Campbell and Eliza Garington, young women of questionable character, were brought up in custody on remand, charged with robbing Benjamin Elsey, and old man, of a purse containing between £6 and £7, in a lodging house, in Finkle Street, where he and his son, a man about thirty, had been staying all night. They pleaded guilty and were sent to prison for two months. The portal said Peggy, again which is short for Margaret and the portal said Ben twice at Greggs Bros.

In November 1876, James Conley and John Murray were charged with assaulting Mary Miller, who kept a common lodging house in the Backway. The portal said Jim, the talker 2 said Mary and at Gregg Bros the portal said John.

In December 1877, Thomas Young was assaulted on Finkle Street by a bulldog-looking character named Parker Ward. The article refers to Finkle Street as hell on earth and that it was sadly a common occurrence.

In July 1878, Mr Suddenly was in the divorce court. His wife had filed for divorce on the grounds of adultery and cruelty. Mr Suddenly had been seen in the company of a woman in a brothel. He had been seen at both Finkle Street and Clayton Street and in the former place there was several houses of ill-fame. Margaret Miller stated that she had formerly resided in Clayton Street, and she had been criminally intimate with the respondent. A woman known as "Lanky Meg" also went to the house and was intimate with the respondent. The portal said Peggy, which is short for Margaret.

In July 1879, James Williams, a stout, elderly man, was sentenced to 14 days for stealing fivepence in coppers from the till of Richard Thompson, Derby Hotel, Tenters Street.

In August 1881, Margaret Hunter was charged with wounding Daniel Gordon. They had both been drinking and got into a quarrel and Hunter took up a razor and inflicted a severe wound on Gordons throat, severing some of the arteries.

In November 1881, Margaret Gilmartin, alias Burt (20), was brought up on a custody charge with stealing a child named Mary Keenan and with causing death by wilfully neglecting to provide proper food. Jane Addison, married woman, Clayton Street gave evidence, along with Jane Ann Alison, occupier of a house of ill-fame in Clayton Street. The portal said Peggy and the Talker 2 at Gregg Bros said Mary.

In the 1881 census, Charles Hird lived at Clayton Street with wife Margaret.   The portal said Peggy.

In the 1881 census, John Jobson lived at 11 market place and was Justice of the Peace, general practitioner, licentiate of society of apothecaries' London. Fellow of the royal college of surgeons and was 71 years of age.

In the 1881 census, Frederick Rollinson, aged 35, lived at High Bondgate and was a soldier. The portal said Freddy.

In the 1881 census, William Smith lived at 3 Fore Bondgate with his family. He was a baker and game dealer and he had a wife called Emily and a son called Wilfred. Shayna picked up Wilfred and I said Willy.

In the 1881 census, William Bradley was a hairdresser and lived at 60 Fore Bondgate. I was given the name Willy.

In March 1885, Robert Jackson, aged 39, of Bondgate, Bishop Auckland, butcher, took his own life by slitting his throat with a cleaver. He had been drinking for a fortnight and was intoxicated the whole time. He was frequently abusive to his wife and children. The portal said Bob.

In 1886, William Potts, Dundas Street, took part in the Bishop Auckland Agricultural Show. The portal said Potts and I picked up the name Willy.

In January 1896, James Sunter, 28, a miner, was charged with unlawfully wounding John Timms. Albert A. Hope, assistant with Dr Ellis said that he had attended the victim and had to put 18 stitches into the wound which extended from about 2 inches behind the lobe of the left ear across the cheek to the opposite side of the upper lip. He had used a pocket knife. He was sentenced to six months hard labour. The portal said Jim and Jack which is another name for John.

In September 1910, there was an advert for loans from Philip Simon 50 Fore Bondgate. The portal said Philip.

In the 1911 census, Charles W. Potts, aged 30, general labourer, Nellie Potts, aged 30, Winifred Potts, aged 3, Frederick Potts, aged 2, and James Potts, aged 1 month lived at 9 Clayton Street which is close to Fore Bondgate. The portal said Eric Potts.

In 1930, Frederick Potts married Florence Iceton at Auckland.

In November 1939, Frederick Taylor, 23, of Newton cap Bank and John Thomas Lyons, 18, of Hawthorn cottages were both sentenced to one month's hard labour imposed at Bishop Auckland Police Court. They were charged with larceny. The portal said Fred and Jack.

In august 1949, John Thomas Lyons, 28, a labourer from Hawthorn cottages was arrested for breaking and entering a house. The portal said Jack which is short for John.

THE TEAPOT THAT DROPPED OFF THE SHELF

MRS COTTONS TEAPOT

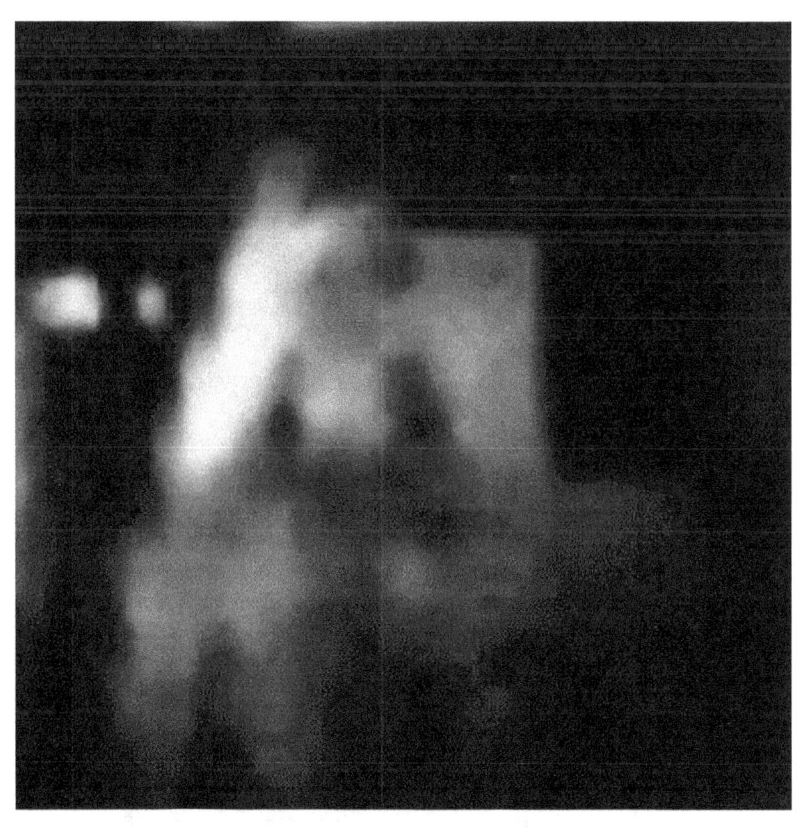

A LADY WATCHING

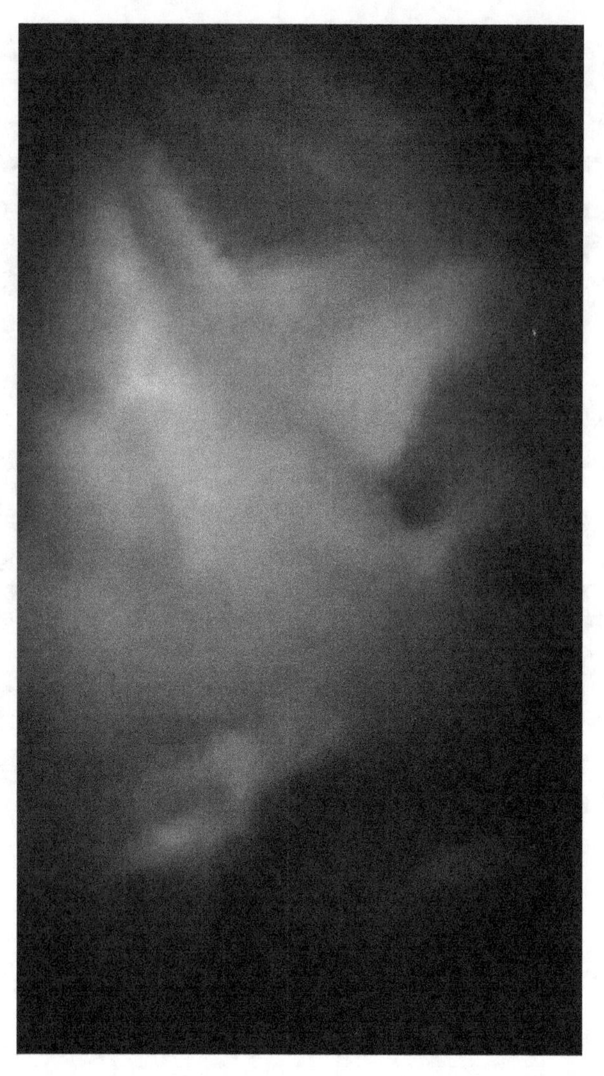

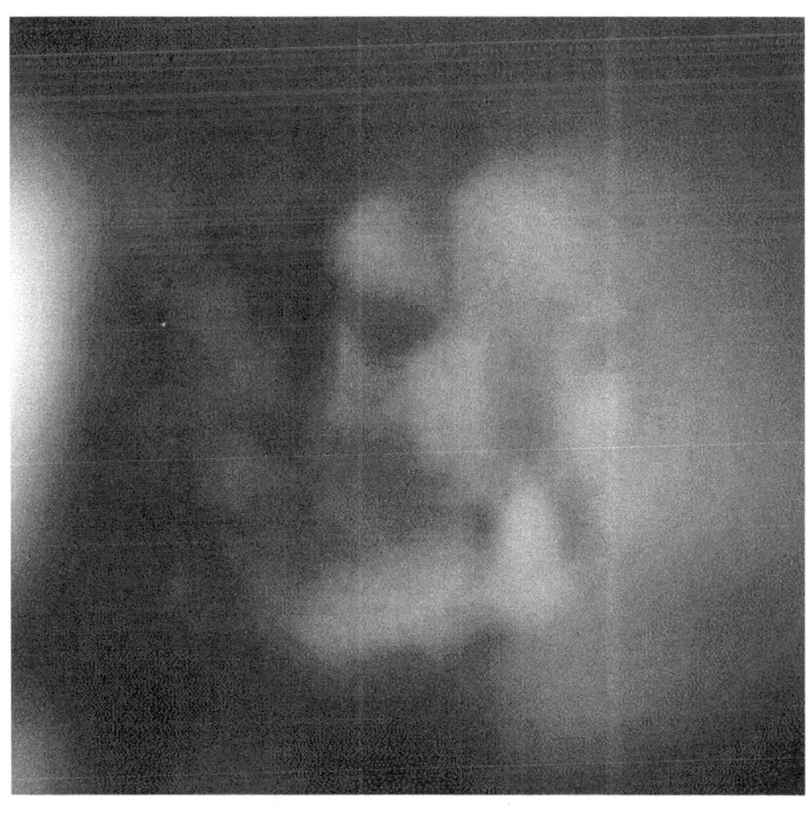

A FIGURE IN THE SHOP

THE FORE BONDGATE AREA

In February 1845, there was a meeting held in the Assembly-room for the purpose of taking into consideration the propriety of petitioning Parliament in favour of the Sunderland, Durham, and Auckland Union Railway.

Elizabeth Robertson was charged by John Race, beer house-keeper, Finkle Street, with refusing to quit his beer house when ordered to do so. This was in 1868.

A woman who was covered with blood was carried by four men down Bondgate and through the busy market place to Dr Hutchinson. This was in 1873.

A police officer was assaulted as he walked up Finkle Street. PC Sluirp was assaulted by someone called Walter when he was attending a disturbance that was going on in the street. This was in 1875.

An alley is also spoken on in Finkle street, which is described as hell upon earth and has villainous looking people always there and fighting and robbing was a common occurrence. This was in 1877.

In December 1879, Dr Barnardo visited the Temperance Hall and delivered an address called "Christian work among Homeless Children."

In May 1883, Jane Ann Allison was fined £10 for keeping a house of ill-fame and harbouring thieves, in Claylon Street, Bishop Auckland.

A father was committed for the manslaughter of his infant and the inquest was at the Derby Hotel. Mr Coroner Dean resumed the inquest and the child was called Jane Coghlan and was 21 months old. This was in 1887.

In March 1888, Maria McDonough, aged twelve years, died suddenly. She complained of pains in the head and shoulders. An inquest was to be held.

In December 1888, before the Auckland bench Elizabeth Hascroft, a married woman belonging to Clayton Street, was charged with disorderly conduct in the Doctors Tunnel. She was under the influence of drink. She had already been cautioned earlier in the evening.

Patrick Clinton, aged 66, died at Finkle Street in December 1892.

There seemed to have been a business on George street that sold everything you could think of and you could get credit/loans, this was featured in an article in 1894.

At Hall Terrace, Henry, son of Mr Johnson Pickering aged 6 years died in October 1901.

Henry Taylor and Jane Taylor, husband and wife, of Finkle street were summoned for assaulting Ann slater in 1905. They were featured in the 1911 census and were still together. They lived with their children Oliver and Henry.

In the 1911 census, Charles William Mordue, a horse keeper lived at 15 Finkle street with his mother Elizabeth and his grandchildren Maria and Mary.

There was an alleged disorderly house in George street and a lady called Frances English was fined. She lived at George street in 1930.

There was a Mrs Humphry's of 16 George street that gave birth to a daughter in 1937.

In august 1949, John Thomas Lyons, 28, a labourer from Hawthorn cottages was arrested for breaking and entering a house.

In March of 1963, the Bishop Auckland and district choral society had Owen Brannigan. Owen Brannigan was given an OBE in 1964. The choral society are still going today.

In 1970, White Brothers had a garage selling Reliant bond bugs and rebel 4 wheelers. Was this the same building?

BONDGATE

The Bishop Auckland races and cock fighting were advertised in July 1736.

Simon Lackenby was a weaver in Bishop Auckland in March 1739.

In May 1749, there was a newspaper article regarding the Bishop Auckland Turnpike. There was a meeting with the trustees at Mrs Dorothy Carr's Talbot pub. There were several inhabitants of Bishop Auckland allowed to compound for going thro' Newgate Barr, The Black Boy and Coundon-Lane Side Barr's. there were also inhabitants of Staindrop, for going thro' Staindrop Barr, and the inhabitants of Coundon and Coundon Grange for going thro' the same Side Barrs. The meeting was regarding repairing the roads.

Two large dwelling houses went up for auction in October 1852. It was occupied by Mr Hutchinson, a surgeon and Mr Robinson, a colliery viewer.

John Edwin Marshall was clerk of the court at Bishop Auckland in March 1853. And one of the judges at Bishop Auckland court house was Henry Stapylton, esq.

A freehold house and Shop situated in Fore Bondgate was put up for auction. It was occupied by Mr John Elwin, grocer. And Two cottages, in Back Bondgate were up for auction at the same time. They were occupied by William Graham, Margaret Wilson and others. This was in November 1853.

James Garry, a shoemaker in Back Bondgate, was at insolvent debtors court in January 1854.

An old established Inn called The Fleece went up for sale or let in Fore Bondgate. It was occupied by Mr John Hall in August 1855.

A.D. Allason was a seedsman and florist in Fore Bondgate in October 1856.

The Three Tuns public house with Three cottages behind, situated in Fore Bondgate, which were occupied by Mrs Longstaff, Mrs Shaw, Mrs Milburn and Mrs Fenwick. Also the Sun Inn, situated in Fore Bondgate, which was occupied by Mr John Hinde, all building went up for auction in March 1857.

There was an advert for a tallow chandler, that could work a dipping machine. The person advertising was called Thomas Lalon, Back Bondgate in November 1857. A tallow chandler was a candle maker. The made candles from tallow (the rendered fat of animals such as cows and sheep).

In 1858, there was an article in the paper about people being drunk at Jane Longstaff's house in Fore Bondgate.

In May 1858, there was a meeting held from the board of health regarding a complaint regarding Mr Edgar wanting to build a wall across the street at Bondgate.

John Hulme, High Bondgate, made an application for a spirit license to his house. This was in September 1858.

Three cottages situated at the top of Back Bondgate Street went up for auction in March 1859. They were occupied by Geo. Earnshaw and others.

In November 1859, there was an serious accident in Bishop Auckland. The wife of James Hardy, a miner, went to Bishop Auckland to make her marketing and indulged rather freely in creature comforts; amongst her purchases were 2lbs of blasting gunpowder for the use of her husband, which was tied to the side of the basket carried on her arm. Her business being concluded, on her way out of town she called at the Edinbro' Castle public house for a last glass of beer and a light for her pipe, and had only got a few yards from the door when a spark from the pipe exploded the gunpowder, setting fire to her dress, and burning her side and arm in a dreadful manner; she was immediately taken into the Sun Inn, and proper remedies applied. The cause of the accident had not cured her of her love for tobacco, as, whilst her wounds were being dressed, she made frequent applications for her pipe. She was furnished with a "rig out" of clothes by the charitable neighbours of the landlady, and taken home to Etherley in a conveyance.

In January 1863, Shepherds Inn was to let. The present tenant was John Moor and the owner was James Thompson Esq.

In July 1866, an inquest was opened before Mr W. D. Trotter, coroner, at the Police Station Bishop Auckland, on the body of George Mills, who died from the effects of the injuries received at an explosion. The incident took place in the warehouse of Mr James Nevison, grocer, in Newgate Street, in which 25lbs of gunpowder exploded. Mills, after blaming a boy named Rutherford in connection with the occurrence, had since died. Rutherford was also really injured in the explosion.

A murderous attack followed a christening at an Irish house, in Back Bondgate, where Michael Shanley, and four brothers named John, Patrick, James and William Donohue were guests. As Shanley left to set off for home he was followed and attacked by the Donohues and other men. This was supposed to have been rivalry over a love affair between Shanley and one of the brothers. This was in November 1869.

A child, 2 ½ years old, named Catherine Summers, died in Back Bondgate in November 1871. She had "toddled" into a neighbour's house and fell into a pan of boiling water which was on a stand on the floor.

In October 1872, Mary Ann Cottons crimes came to light in West Auckland. The accused, a middle-aged woman, about 5th 6" in height and of rather swarthy complexion was arrested with the wilful murder of her stepson, Charles Edward Cotton. Mary Ann and Frederick lived at Walbottle near Newcastle but had quarrelled with some of the neighbours, who accused her of poisoning a number of pigs. The family moved to West Auckland where Frederick obtained work at the colliery close by. They lived a quiet and peaceful life for about five months when the husband died suddenly. This was in 19th September 1871 and he was 39 years old. His death was followed quickly by his oldest son Frederick who died on the 12th March aged 10 years old , his youngest son Robert died on the 31st March aged 14 months and the lodger named Joseph Nattrass died on the 3rd April aged 35 years. This left one child, Charles Edward Cotton who died on the 12th July aged 7 years.

A witness who lived opposite her had frequently seen her beat the child. She was very strict with the boy and wouldn't let him play with other children. She often complained about him being an inconvenience to her and even asked the boys uncle to take him in but her refused. She tried to put him into the workhouse but was told that she would have to go in too, but she replied "that is a place I will not go". She also complained that having the boy at the house was stopping her from taking in a respectable lodger. There was a rumour in the village that the lodger would be Mr Mann and she had plans to marry him and the witness asked her if it was true. She smiled and said it might be so, but this boy (pointing to Charles) was in the way. But she also remarked "of course, he will never be able to get up; he will go like the rest of the Cotton family" and the witness responded "oh, nonsense; he is a fine, healthy, little fellow". On the following Friday, the witness was walking up the village, Mary Ann appeared at her own door and said "my boy has just died" and he went to inform the police. This caused suspicion in the village, as the boy had been healthy the week before.

As the witness was questioned he mentioned that when Joe had been poorly he had mentioned that "if I was only better, I would be out of this" and died four days later after being looked after by Mary Ann. Four days before his death May Ann's youngest child died. She deferred the burial and when she was asked about it, she told the witness "I am going to put it off until Joe dies. He has gone upstairs now, and, poor fellow, he will never come down until they carry him feet first."

The day before his death he had told the doctor that apart from the grinding pain in his stomach, there was nothing wrong with him. He died in a convulsive fit, the same way as her husband and children.

The inquest of the deaths were natural causes but this caused dissatisfaction in the village and Dr Kilburn was induced to make another examination. He had buried a portion of Charles Edwards stomach in his garden and this detected arsenic. He informed the police and she was apprehended. She was examined at Bishop police court and charged with Wilful murder.

The exhumation of the bodies of Frederick Cotton Snr, Frederick Cotton Jnr and Robert Robson were proceeded in July 1872 but only the bodies of the children could be found. Nearly a dozen graves, of which records appeared to have been kept, had been opened but the search for the prisoners late husband was abandoned. The exhumation of the other Three bodies was ordered by the Bishop Auckland magistrates and the work of disinterment in St Helen's churchyard began as early as 5am. The coffins of the Two children were soon discovered, and being removed to an empty house near to the church and the bodies dissected by the medical gentleman present. Traces of an irritant poison were found throughout the whole of the viscera. The search for the body of Frederick Cotton were given up a few minutes before 1pm.

Additional charges again Mary Ann Cotton who was at the time in Durham Gaol awaiting trial for the murder of her step son Charles Edward Cotton, and who was accused of poisoning Two of her other children, her husband and a lodger at the same place a few months before, was to be investigated at Bishop Auckland over the course of a few days. The request for her to be transferred from Durham to Bishop Auckland was received in February 1873.

Mary Ann Cotton was a regular at the Sun Inn that was on Bondgate. She was remanded in custody to the police station on Bondgate, near to the pub and her committal proceedings were held in the Bondgate court before she was committed to trial at the Durham Spring Assizes. Whilst the trial was on a break, she was taken to the Sun Inn. Did we communicate with Mrs Cotton once again?

At the Bishop Auckland police court, James Conner, an Irishman was charged with cutting and wounding William Payne. Mr Payne, a pitman, was proceeding from Fore Bondgate to his house when his attention was drawn to a quarrel and the prisoner was striking his own mother. He then started to assault Mr Payne. This was in July 1873.

At the police court William Elliott, a putter at West Auckland Colliery, pleaded guilty to a charge of having cruelly ill-treated a pony in the pit. He was seen beating a pony about its fore-parts with a pick-shaft. He was fined in in January 1879.

Mr Thompson, manager of the Kings Arms Inn Newgate street, was riding a horse across the market place and the horse reared and seriously injured him. The horse belonged to Mr Dodds. This was in January 1879.

At Bishop Auckland Police Court, Elizabeth Scanlon, a girl of about Fifteen years of age was charged with stealing a piece of carpet from Margaret Smith of Back Bondgate. She was sentenced to Fourteen days imprisonment with hard labour. This was in September 1879.

A fire, which caused extensive damage, broke out in the candle manufactory of Mr Watson, situated in Back Bondgate. The building was leased by Mr Baker in April 1881.

In January 1886, a train passing from Durham to Bishop Auckland, whilst passing through Bondgate tunnel, knocked down and killed an elderly man.

Dr McCullagh, the medical officer of health for the Bishop Auckland local board, said that his annual report for the town was anything but pleasant or satisfactory reading. It was regarding the sewerage and sanitation of the town. The death rate for 1893 was 22.8 and in 1892 was 19.04. The infant mortality was at the rate of 161.2 per thousand, the average for England and Wales being 149. Deaths from zymotic diseases numbered 47. The death rate was very high, being 4.47, as against 1.9 the previous year. The increase was due to a large number of fatal cases of typhoid fever and diarrhoea. Typhoid (enteric) fever was fatal in 17 instances. He had investigated 106 cases and in several houses there were serious sanitary defects, such as untapped drains, waste pipes that were not disconnected, ashpits and privies built again walls of dwelling rooms. He believed that the primary cause was the pollution of water supply by sewage infected with typhoid and that the disease was further propagated by the entrance of infected sewer gas into houses due to undisinfected ashpits and privies. This report made special mention of Fore Bondgate and Back Bondgate in February 1894.

William Brand, a youth, of Back Bondgate was brought up in the custody of Sergeant Oxnard, charged under the Criminal Law Amendment Act with the intention of having carnal knowledge of Jane Hinds, a girl aged 13. This was in March 1896.

John Dennison, a property owner who used to be an Inn keeper, was summoned by Thomas Lowe on a charge of assaulting him in Powell's Yard, Back Bondgate. He struck him over the head with a whip. Mary Elizabeth Dodds was a witness. This was in April 1898.

At the Auckland Petty Session, Mary Hind, a good-looking young woman was charged with wounding Jas. Kennedy in Back Bondgate. She threw a pint pot at him and split his head open. As he fell to the ground she grabbed a poker and struck him over the head with it. This was in September 1899.

George Bradley, Innkeeper of the Crown Inn, Back Bondgate, was summoned by Supt. Daley on a charge of permitting drunkenness In December 1902.

In September 1910, there was an advert for loans from Philip Simon 50 Fore Bondgate.

A woman was sentence to two months imprisonment at Bishop Auckland Police Court charged with stealing £30 from the Spirit Vaults at Bondgate where she formerly worked voluntarily. Jennie E. Bayles, aged 36, was a widow with Two children. She had stolen the money from Mary Teresa Gillett. This was in March 1939.

There was a report in a newspaper regarding the repairs to the roads in North Bondgate. It stated that Fore Bondgate was a narrow road and two cars struggled to pass (it's still the same now). It also stated that North Bondgate which ran parallel and joined Fore Bondgate near the police station. This was in July 1939.

In December 1932, Mrs H. Wilson lived at 50 Fore Bondgate.

THE WELCOME INN

I came across the Welcome Inn when I was doing research for the Snooker Club for our 2nd Book on Bishop Auckland. It was in a newspaper article from the early 1900s, and although I didn't read it I then knew that the pub was really old.

I contacted the pub to see about having a public event there and Kelsey said yes straight away. We set a date but unfortunately we had to postpone it as the pandemic hit. We waited until everything with Covid19 had calmed down and rearranged. The date that we picked clashed with England playing Germany in the Euro 2021 football tournament which meant that the night we had picked, when the pub would be closed, had to be changed again.

We rearranged for a date in July and it nearly got postponed again as Kelsey had badly hurt her ribs. She asked if we could postpone it again but unfortunately we didn't have a date free in the diary so we went ahead with it.

I had never been in the pub before and had to have a practice run at finding it, its hidden away in-between houses.

The day of the investigation, when I was getting the kit ready I got the big bag of Victorian dolls out and was about to put them back when I little voice in my head told me to take them. I then had a feeling that the building was linked or close to a children's home. I'm so pleased that I took them as the children ended up being a very important part of the night.

We made our way to the Welcome and Hannah couldn't make it as David was still poorly. Michael met us downstairs and gave us the guided tour of the house upstairs. Kelsey and Michael were having a drink with friends outside whilst we investigated.

We set up CCTV in the living room, landing, pointing up the stairs and 2 in different ends of the bar. We also set up the SLS in the bar and as soon as I set it up I noticed a child sat on a chair watching me.

We were joined by Jo, Joanne, Sheila, Vicky, Simon and Jasmin and it was a lovely number for an investigation.

We started by saying the prayer in the living room and started the investigation upstairs in the living room. Most people had a seat and I leaned again the fireplace and felt like I had to tell a story. Maybe someone used to lean on there.

I asked if anyone was getting anything before I started shouting out. Jo said that the room had a nice feeling and I said that there was a male presence in the building. We caught an EVP on Handy Cam saying 'good'. Shayna felt that she had a tight chest. I said that I felt that someone had gassed themselves. Maybe not in here but in the street.

Shayna wondered if it was a gas explosion and I felt that when I was in here putting the camera in I felt that someone had died by gassing. Sheila asked how old the building is and I said that Kelsey didn't know. Sheila pointed out that it is a gas fire as she could see the pipe from where she was sitting.

I said I wasn't touching it as I might have been getting a premonition of my death! Jasmin was stood near the window in the corner and said that she could feel something around her face. I felt that something was around mine too and didn't know if I had whiskers. Shayna was getting the name William and had a vision of him being like the colonel off KFC. Which started us talking about KFC as I was dieting. Shayna and I both had stomach ache.

I decided to try a portal session.

As I was setting it up I had a slavery mouth and I said that it usually meant a visit from a certain family. Vicky said that she had the pain in her neck again, like she did when we visited Gregg Bros and It was Mrs Cotton.

I said that it usually means that the Cottons are around. Bev said that if it was as old as the Sun Inn she may have visited here. Joanne was getting a pain in her ankle and so was Shayna. Something was also touching Shayna's head.

I turned on the portal.

Tom (lady)

Who's Tom?

We heard voices through the portal and they sounded like children.

Right, hang on and I'll get you right. Let me see which settings are right.

Can you say something to us? Just so that I know that its right.

By 11 (man)

(we were finishing at 11 where they going to do something before then)

Did that call you a loser? (Shayna)

Can you give us you name please?

Fk you! (man)**

Were you a landlord?

I couldn't make it out so changed the settings again.

Shayna said that she had the same carpets years ago.

Liar (man)

Liar! No you never.

Did she have this carpet?

Jasmin said we might sell it.

Dermot (man)

Shayna went on to say where she got it from.

Cheer us up (man)

Did somebody gas themselves in here? or in the area?

The portal turned itself off.

Vicky said that she still had the Knot at the back of her neck.

Have you still got the pain?

Jack (lady)

Shayna felt that she had a problem with her Right ear.

Is Mrs Cotton here?

Yeah (lady)

Someone felt as if someone was getting strangled. I think it was Jasmin but was hard to tell on film.

Get off (child)

Are any of the children here? Are any of the children here? That was totally wrong grammar.

Annie (child)

Keith or leave (child)

Leave? We've just come.

Get out (child)

Was that get out? (Shayna)

Yeah (child)

Yeah.

Are you a child?

***music**

Where you from the children's home.

I meant to bring a doll up here and I've been stood in front of the CCTV

Shall I change the channel? What do you reckon?

I started to get a bad headache and Shayna felt sick.

We caught an EVP of a man saying 'That's what we felt'.

Shayna wondered if there was arsenic behind the wall paper.

I changed the channel on the portal.

Can you give us your name please?

Jack (man)

I can hear you saying something but you are too quiet.

Shayna said to put it on the carpet. I put it on the floor.

Is that better? How's that?

Yes (man)

We've come to learn about you.

We caught an EVP saying 'Martha'.

Can you give us your name?

Are you still there?

Easter (child)

Was that piss off? (Shayna)

Some of the group thought it was.

Are you swearing at me?

I said that it was a gas fire and Shayna felt it could have been carbon monoxide.

Was it an accident?

Bev said to try it on the other channel again.

We caught an EVP saying 'Bob'.

Do you want me to change the channel or do an EVP session.

Michael came in and picked up his phone charger.

Help (lady)

Was that help? (Shayna)

Do you need help with something? It's always help lately. What do you need help with? Is it the same person?

Vicky went all cold down one side.

Aye (lady)

Is your surname Mowbray? We caught an EVP of a man saying 'Parchment'.

Is this Isabella? We caught an EVP of a child giggling and then sniffing.

I started to feel slavery mouthed and Jasmin was feeling cold.

Shayna asked if my shoulder blade was sticking out and I said it shouldn't be!

Shayna said that I looked like I had a hump and Jasmin and Sheila could both see it.

Have I got a hump? It is spondylosis.

Did you have spondylosis?

Step back or Steph had (man)

Sort your posture out! (Shayna)

Something's tickling my arm. (Bev)

I have gooseplmples all down my Right leg. (Jasmin)

I changed the channel again.

Can you do something for me?

Are you near Jasmin?

Alex (child)

Can you give me your name?

Jasmin could feel a little arm around her.

We decided to try an EVP session.

I asked anyone had any funny feelings before I started calling out. Jasmin said that there was definitely a child wrapping its arm around her leg and I said we would try to find out who it was.

If there are any spirits in the room with us can you come forward and talk into this microphone here? Is there a child wrapping themselves around Jasmin's leg? Jasmin's the weirdo stood in the corner. We caught an EVP of a man saying 'let go'. Are there any spirit people here, are there any children here? Is it the child that was downstairs? Can you come and tell me your name or tap on the microphone if you like? There was a small tap caught.

If you are a child and you are in this room, you can come and talk to us you know. We won't tell you off. We aren't here to harm you. Were you from the children's home? Or did you live here? were you the child from downstairs? Can you knock one of those dollies off downstairs whilst we are up here. Was anybody poisoned? Can you just tell us by tapping on the microphone.

People noticed that there was a ticking noise on the recordings and we thought it was my watch. I recorded my watch close to it and there was a ticking. Shayna said that I should get down on the floor and try again and we caught a very distinctive EVP of a man saying 'down here'. but at the time some of the team thought it was German. Sheila was given the name Howard and didn't know why.

Who was the man who has just been talking to us? We have caught you on voice recorder and we would like your name please? Is it Howard? I'm impressed where you plucked that little number from. Is Howard here with us?

We talked for a little while about if it was German that we couldn't really understand what was said. Joanne said that she knew a little bit of German.

Are you German? Can you speak to me in German please? I can't answer you back in German but I'd like to listen to you. Were you a prisoner of war? When you were released did you live here? A lot of them settled here didn't they?

Is there anybody here that would like to talk to us before we go? We are going to move to a different room. And I would like to talk to the man who spoke really clearly into the microphone. Can you speak to me again? I had a neck problem going on and Shayna had a bad shoulder. Vicky problem had gone now. Did you pass from a hanging? Can you tell me that? I know it's awful to talk about. But now is the time for you to tell your story, whatever that is. Can you give us your name?

Can I just ask is that Mrs Cotton? We caught a very feint EVP saying 'yes'. Have you come to talk to us tonight? Did you drink in here? I know you liked to drink at the Sun Inn. But maybe you came in here. Shayna asked if it was a brothel. Was it a brothel? We caught an EVP saying 'no'.

We started to talk a little bit about the buildings in the area. I didn't really know much about the station and things that passed. We also talked about the teapot at beamish and how there was one in Labyrinth.

Was the lady with the hump, the lady that looked after the children at Mrs Cottons former home? She was bad with Arthritis?

We moved into the kitchen, taking the bear with us. I decided to try the talker 2 as it had been really successful when we investigated Hexham.

'Mary, Elaine, your there, your ?, they are merged.'

I asked if the children were there. 'They're here.'

Is Isabella here? 'They are not you.'

We caught an EVP of a cat.

'We know you.'

'They going to know you.'

'There's William.'

'They're leaving.'

Did somebody gas themselves? Is the question too hard?

Do you want to do some table tipping?

'They are here.'

'They want to find you.'

'They are allowed.'

'They were murdered.'

'The rug.'

'Children's home in the area.'

'Murder.'

We talked about how good the Talker2 worked at Vane Tempest Hall too.

We caught an EVP of a child.

We went back into the living room to try table tipping before going downstairs.

Jo and Joanne sat at the table and I put the bear in the middle of the table. Joanne said she was wary of the bear following Spennymoor WMC when the spirits wouldn't let her put it down.

The table was moving immediately as soon as they sat down. And the bears paw was flashing. I moved around to the other side with the Handy Cam.

I started asking questions in the hope of getting the table to move in response.

Is this a man? No. Is it a lady? No. Is it a child? The table was being knocked from underneath. I asked if it was a boy or a girl and it responded as girl. It knocked again.

Did you live here? No.

Were you at the children's home? There was a tap.

So you lived at the children's home. Were you very young when you passed to spirit. Where you younger than 10? There was a tap.

Can you give us your name. is it a Elizabeth? Shayna asked if it was Annabelle. Joanne asked if it was Darcy? Do you know Darcy? The Handy Cam tapped.

Were you both at the children's home? Or did you meet in the spirit world? The table was moving and the Handy Cam tapped.

I asked if they could use everybody's energy and knock the bear off.

So, you were at the children's home? Did you have any brothers or sisters? Were you on your own? Still no response.

Do you know Joanne? No response.

What was it like at the children's home? Was it awful? I know it's probably not great to talk about. Did you have lots of friends there? Did you not like it? Did you have any visitors?

Shayna felt the meals were like slop.

Was it the 1800s when you were there? I was sure the head on the bear moved.

Was it the 1900s or do you not know? We felt she didn't know. There was a tap on the Handy Cam.

Was it close to here? There was a tap on the Handy Cam.

Was it the one at the end of the road or is it closed now?

Is it still open?

Shayna got 2 dates. 1912 and 1945.

Was it any of those dates?

Joanne asked if it was 1912. I said they might not know.

They wondered if it was the school on Etherley lane.

Did you go to that school or was it definitely a children's home.

Will I be able to find you in the census? How will I know your name?

Is your name Elizabeth? No.

Is it Annabelle? Charlotte? Bella?

There was a tap underneath the table for Bella.

Hello Bella, I'm going to look for you. It'll be a long job but I will look.

It's not Isabelle is it. It was a yes. Joanne was covered in goose pimples.

Is this Isabella Mowbray? Or just Isabelle.

Are you related to Mrs Cotton. It was a definite no.

Your Isabelle, not related to Mrs Cotton. It was a yes.

Are you a different Isabelle that comes to visit me? No.

Are you the same one? Did we talk a couple of weeks ago? There was a tap.

Were you poisoned? Were you given something nasty in your food or in your tea? It was a yes.

Have you come with any of your brothers or sisters Isabelle? Yes.

Are they all here? What's brought you here? Just because we are here? Have you just come to talk because we are quite friendly now aren't we? It was a no.

Are we not friendly?

Bev asked if she could tip the table towards the fire and the table tipped.

I asked her if she could make the bears head move.

Have you got something to say? Do you know who the man was who spoke to me before? No.

Is he just from here? You don't know him. Because we don't know him either.

Was he German? Thats probably too hard a question.

Was he foreign? Yes.

Did he talk funny?

I was sure the bear was turning towards me. I asked her to frighten Bev to death as she hates it.

Can you make the arms move? I asked if she was still there and the table was vibrating.

I asked her to get all of her friends together and make it move. The table was creaking at this point.

I asked if I should put the portal on.

If I put the portal on as well as the table you might get some energy off it.

Joanne had a pain in her right eye.

Are you turning the head really slowly. Are you hiding underneath the table? Can you lift it?

Joanne asked her to knock really loudly on the bottom of the table so everyone could hear it.

I asked Bev to come over to me so that she could see the bear. It looked like it had a tear in its eye.

I had never seen it before and it looked like it had a tear. I said it probably didn't but I had been looking at it for 10 minutes and hadn't noticed it before.

Are you making the bear cry? Bev will definitely hate the bear now!

The bear definitely looked teary eyed. Are you making it cry? Are you sad?

Bev said the teddy was possessed and there was a tap.

I heard someone say 'awe' and asked the group if it was them. They said it wasn't and it was caught on Handy Cam.

Hi, its lovely to see you?

I heard another voice and thought I was going nuts.

Was that you? Its lovely to see you. Are you making my bear cry? Do you like my bear? Is that what you came to see? The bear?

We didn't have the bear when we visited your house. we didn't have it did we? I bet you would have liked me to have took the bear.

Is this a different Isabelle? Yes.

Were you from Bishop Auckland before you went to the children's home.

Or were you brought here? Yes.

Was it far away? Was it a village nearby? Yes.

Shayna wondered if her mum was a prostitute.

Were you taken away from your mummy? Yes.

Did someone come and take you away from your mummy? Yes.

So your mummy didn't die? Yes.

So your mummy died and you were taken away? Yes.

What about your daddy? Did your daddy die? No.

You were taken from your daddy? Yes.

Did your daddy not cope? Did your daddy like a drink? Did he not work? Could he not afford to keep you? No.

Was your daddy around? Yes.

Bev felt that she saw a white outline of a child near to the table and we caught a glimpse on Handy Cam. I took a screenshot and it looked like a blonde little girl stood near to Joanne.

I said it was lovely to talk to her and she could play with the dolls downstairs. I asked if it was the girl downstairs and she said it was.

I asked if she was moving the head and Joanne said the ear moved.

I asked if she had anything to say. Joanne asked if she was wondering what we were all doing there.

Did you just pop in and say hello?

Are you always here?

Shayna was getting the name Margot.

Do you know a Margot? No.

We felt that the child had gone. And we wondered if she was downstairs.

We headed downstairs for a break .

We ended the session and Simon and Jasmin had a go at the table in the end near where the SLS was.

Simon said that if the bear turned to look at him he would die.

I did some calling out asking if there was any spirits in the room could they move the table. I was sure the bear was moving. Sheila was keeping an eye on the bear as she could see it past Simons shoulder.

I asked spirit to tap on the table. I asked if there were any children with us. The table was starting to move and I asked if they could rock it from side to side. There was a couple of really loud thuds caught on Handy Cam.

I asked if there was somebody with us that was very sad. I said that I felt very sad and Sheila reminded me that I said that earlier on in the evening. I also asked if something sad had happened in the part where we felt sadness and Shayna felt it was a linked to a male.

I asked them to tell me something about the pub that no one knows. Shayna wondered if there was a fire.

I asked if somebody was murdered or killed there. And the table moved.

I asked who was murdered and was it a fight? Was somebody stabbed as Sheila was getting that earlier. Shayna asked if someone was glassed. I could see the energy starting to build underneath the table.

I asked if it was a man and the table started to twist.

So a man was murdered? Was he murdered by another man? It looked like they were started to tip it onto 2 legs.

Was it a fight? It wasn't an Irish family was it?

There was an EVP on Handy Cam saying 'I know'.

Was there an Irish family fight or was there an Irish family involved? No.

Was it someone who used to drink here? Someone from the area?

Was it outside? Yes.

We caught an EVP saying 'no' and it was a lady.

So not necessarily the pub but someone in the street.

We caught an EVP saying 'F**king hell my photo'.

Have we spoken to you before?

Shayna felt that he ran over a bridge. Went from this area and went to the town.

Sheila felt that they were stabbed and I asked if they ran over the bridge.

Jo said there was a new bridge.

Did they make off towards the town? The table moved.

Simon said that were the road is was the railway lines. I asked if it happened at the railway lines.

How will I know it's you? Will I be able to find you?

Simon said his hands were hurting.

Was it a gang fight? Was it a fight and you were caught up in it? Was it a night out went wrong? We caught an EVP of a man saying 'yes'.

Was it over a woman? We caught an EVP saying 'yes'.

Was it over money? Was it just rival gangs or something? The table moved.

Was it just lads being lads and went a bit far? Too much to drink and ended in a bad way? Were you drinking in here and it went outside? The table was lifting.

Was it a long time ago?

Jasmin kept seeing flashing lights underneath the table.

Was it less than 20 years ago? EVP 'no'.

More than 20 year ago? EVP 'yes'.

More than 50 years ago? It was moving.

More than 100 years ago? There was a tap.

More than 150 years ago? Nothing.

So you are looking at early 1900's and it moved.

Shayna remembered 1912 and 1945. There was a tap.

I asked if they wanted to get a message to somebody or just popped in to be remembered?

Or are you just wanting to get yourself in a book?

We caught the same man saying 'I love that book'

Awe well at least you'll be remembered if you're in a book.

Were you sad? Is that why I'm feeling sad? Do you know the children upstairs? No.

Were you the man that spoke into my voice recorder? No.

We asked if it was Kelsey's grandad.

I felt that it was someone else now.

Were you young? Were you a teenager? No.

Were you in your 20s? No.

Were you in your 30s? No.

Were you in your 40s? No we felt that he had gone.

Was there a fire here? No.

Can you tell me something about the children's home? Why did I have to bring all of these dolls?

We joked about leaving the creepy dolls laid about to scare Michael and I said we should hang one by a rope. We caught an EVP saying 'aye that'.

I said I was only joking.

We ended the session and tried an EVP session.

Is the spirit that was here with us, moving the table, that was stabbed, are you still here? If you are can you talk into this please? Can you give me your name?

Can you tell me if it happened outside?

Can you tell me something about this pub that we don't know?

Are you Kaitlin's grandad and are you German?

I asked the team if they wanted to know anything else and Joanne said that she didn't say anything at the time but as Shayna mentioned a fire earlier she saw what looked like heat in the living room. She was looking at the carpet an saw it moving like when air gets hot above a radiator. She thought it was her eyes but now wonders if she was picking it up from spirit.

If that are any spirit in the room with us can you let me know if there's been a fire? Has there been a fire in this building? I don't mean a coal fire, I mean a fire. Did it burn down or was there a fire in one of the rooms? We caught an EVP of man and I think he says 'at the time'.

Are there any landlords here that want to talk to us? Even if its to tell us to get out?

Shayna wondered if it was arson so I asked if it was done on purpose. On voice recorder we caught an EVP saying 'yeah'.

Can you tell me something really juicy about this place? I know there was a lot of prostitution and there were brothels but can you tell me anything else?

Did you police get called to here? Was one of the landlords arrested? We were seeing shadows close to us? Are you in the corner looking? You can come and sit next to Sheila, she doesn't bite. She's on fire tonight!

We decided to move around to the other side of the bar. Simon took the bear. I decided to take some photos and asked Bev to. I said that I would do some calling out and see if I could get them to touch something as we had lot of trigger objects in the room and said that I thought that they were shy and didn't want to talk to us. Shall I try the table?

Vicky was chasing after the moth and killed it. I went on the table with Shayna. I said I wouldn't get too excited as it doesn't work for me usually.

The table was moving immediately and we weren't asking any questions. It was trying to twist the table. I could see the energy around the bear in the middle. Bev asked if she could join us.

The table started to tip towards Bev and Shayna asked it to knock the bear off. I asked if they could do something really impressive like tip it over onto 2 legs or spin it on one like a ballerina? Then it tipped over and I asked if they could see how low they could get it without knocking it on to the floor. We were held tipped right over and I said I couldn't stay like this long as it really hurt. It was going right to the floor and I asked it to bring it back up but it just stood there in mid-air.

Jo asked if they did that on purpose and I think it did.

Shayna backed out and Bev and I tried again. I said that I would have a hump in my back now. I asked if they could see if they could do it with just the two of us. We caught an EVP of a girl saying 'just the two of them'.

Do you like Bev's posh nails? You can tell she doesn't do a proper job! The table was moving and I asked them to twist it or make it dance on one leg? Is this a child? I started to get earache in my left ear. Shayna said she had it in her right earlier.

Have you got a bad ear? Or have you had a clip around the ear?

Shayna asked if it was a cauliflower ear but I said it just hurst like it was an infection.

I asked if they were still there and Bev asked them to tip the table. It started to tip towards me very slowly.

Well hello. Is it because you want to get me off my chair? Do you think it's funny?

It started to tip again and I was on my feet. Don't make me go all the way down there! It was on two legs and I asked if they could spin it on one leg.

Bev said that they just wanted to make the table drop and it dropped. It really hurt!

I asked if anyone else wanted a go as my back was done. I saw a shadow move and Sheila said that she saw a shadow in the passage. It was like someone had stepped into the room and Jasmin caught a dark figure on her phone.

Jo and Joanne started a table tipping session and opted to sit opposite us. Jo said that something was scratching with nails underneath the table. It was a bit unnerving for them and I put the voice recorder underneath the table asking them not to tip the table towards me.

I laid on the floor with the microphone underneath the table. It was still scratching but it was very quiet on the voice recorder.

Joanne asked them if they were scratching underneath the table and if they could do it again.

Jo asked if it was a child and I could feel static around my hand as I was laid under but she didn't think it was a child. She asked if it was a man and if he lived there. There was a tap and an EVP saying 'yes'.

So you live here? Tap.

I take it were you a landlord? Tap.

Or did you live here before it was a pub. Was it just a house or was there something on this land before it was a pub? Yes.

Jo asked if they died on the railway. The table moved. Did you die on the railway track?

Shayna asked if it was ever a railway house.

Jo asked if they worked on the railway. Tap.

Bev started to choke and made us all jump. I asked if she had swallowed the moth.

Joanne asked if they worked on a train. It was going towards Joanne.

She asked if they used to drive a train. Or was it a fireman?

Jo asked if he was an engineer and did he help build trains. She said that Morrison's was built on the works.

Joanne was on her feet. Jo asked if they could tip it towards Joanne. I was still laid on the floor.

Joanne carried on asking questions. I asked If it was an accident? The table moved.

Jo asked if they could twist it on one leg and make it go around. Joanne asked if they have spoked to other people tonight and if they had spoken to people before. The table was handing in mid-air again and I said that they can't do that as it really hurts. I felt that someone had a wicked sense of humour.

It finally tipped!

Whilst the table was on the floor, we turned it upside down to check underneath for scratches. We couldn't really make anything out. I decided to have a walk around the bar towards the SLS machine and noticed that the little figure was sat on the stool again. I pointed out to the group that you could see me on the monitor but you could also see a smaller figure sat. I waved at the spirit and asked them to wave back at me and it did! I was waving and saying hello and we caught an EVP on Handy Cam of a child saying 'hello'. As we all stood and watched it looked like another child had joined the spirit sitting on the stool as there looked to be 4 legs now, like one was sat on the other.

I noticed the time and went over to where the portal was placed and did a final portal session.

Our house (man)

Our house? Do you live here?

Live here (man)

It's been loved talking to you.

We caught an EVP of a man saying 'careful'.

You haven't minded us being here have you?

Moved in (man)

Ok? We don't mind being ok. It's good that you can talk to us.

Are the children OK?

Ivor (man)

Return (man)

Joanne said that she had a bad eye.

Have you got a bad eye? What's happened to this eye? What happened to it?

Were you injured?

He left (man)

Did you have an injury and hurt your head? It's not the man from the railway is it?

Did you have an accident?

I did (man)

Did you hit your head off the railway lines or something?

Axel (man)

Harold (man)

Did you have an accident on the track?

Joanne said about the trains used to go past the pub to go to Willington.

Joanne said that the sidings were close where they kept the carriages and the works were further up the street.

Did you work at the works?

I did (man)

Joanne (man)

Joanne said her uncle would have been responsible for his own length of the railway. They used to win awards for their length of railway.

Jack (man)

Jack? Jo knew a jack but Joanne's uncle was called John but got called Jack.

Joanne said that he lived at Shildon and I wondered if he worked at the works but she didn't know much about him.

Is this another message for Joanne?

Michael came through and said that there wouldn't be any sleep in the building!

Did jack work at the railway works? Shildon shops?

He did (man)

Most people who lived at Shildon had something to do with the railways.

Jo said that the workers from the railway lived in the rows of houses and that if you lived at Princess Street you had a good job. It even had a church and was like a community.

I said that I loved learning things about Bishop Auckland.

The dentist (man)

Joanne said that they got prizes for their part of the railway and got a sign saying prize length.

We have to go home but its lovely that you have talked to us.

Pleasure (man)

Thank you very much its being nice to talk to you. We have learned a bit about the railways and bit about you.

Are you going to make sure that the kids are alright?

Today (man)

Right, thank you very much. Goodnight.

Are you going to say goodnight?

Champion (man)

Champion? That's do.

I'm Bill (man)

Bill? We have to go now.

Harding (man)

Will I find you?

Kaitlin's grandad was caught Bill and he was German.

Nice to hear from Bill. We have to go so you will have to talk to us again?

Goodnight.

We turned the portal off and finished the investigation.

Everyone agreed that it had been an amazing night but we didn't realise that we had caught so many EVPs during the night.

I think that Michael and Kaitlin got a bit of a shock at the amount of evidence that was caught, but remember they hadn't yet moved in!!!

RESEARCH

In December 1744, the Dwelling house of Alexnder Walker of Bishop Auckland was broken into by Thomas Earnshaw and George Earnshaw. An appeal was placed for the return of the stolen goods or apprehension of the men and a reward was offered. The portal said Alex.

In February 1870, The Royal Alfred Theatre was situated in the Welcome Inn Grounds. The address was William Race, The Welcome Inn. Was this Bill?

In February 1870, Hannah Dodd's was charged with stealing jewellery whilst living at Mr William Race's The Welcome Inn. She worked as a servant.

In November 1872, a great amnesty meeting was held in the Welcome Inn field. Many distinguished Irishmen attended the meeting as a deputation from the Amnesty Association of Dublin.

Thomas Forster was charged with unlawfully wounding Ralph Gilchrist in a brothel in Finkle street. This was featured in an article in 1875. The portal said Tom.

In 1877, Mr William Armstrong, aged 68 and Mr William Atkinson, aged 31 died at Waldron Street. The portal said Bill.

In July 1877, John Toman and John Hall, two respectable young men surrendered to their bail to answer a charge of unlawfully assaulting John Stockport at Bishop Auckland. The two men were throwing stones at Stockport and one of which knocked his eye out. Joanne had a problem with her eye and the portal said Jack, which is a nickname for John.

In October 1877, there was a gas explosion in Tenters Street. It was the house of Dr. Arnold and he had only recently moved there. He could smell gas. He lit and candle and searched the house for the source when there was a huge explosion. Although stunned he went into the cellar to turn off the gas. Windows were blown out, the pantry roof was raised. Dr Arnold was burned on the face and hands. Shayna felt there was a fire and I was aware of gas.

In March 1878, Mr John Henderson, ex-Superintendent of the police, died at his home at Waldron Street. The portal said Jack. Was this John?

In October 1881, a handicap was held at the Welcome Inn ground.

In February 1881, Thomas Quinn, 17 years of age, residing in Grainger Street, met with his death in a shocking manner. He worked at the brick works connected with Newton Cap Colliery and because entangled and was drawn in between the wheels and was fearfully lacerated. The portal said Tom.

In May 1885, opened the home of destitute children at Waldron Street. Mr Joseph Lingford opened the home and it comprised two large dwelling houses. Mr Lingford had placed Mr and Mrs Robert Rutherford in charge. The children taken in must be orphans and would be looked after until they were 15 years of age and at that time they would be put into service.

In June 1885, John Jackson, The Welcome Inn, was charged with keeping open for the sale of liquor. Sergeant White in plain clothes entered the pub and saw him hand a woman a wicker-cased stone bottle of beer. The portal said Jack.

In December 1885, there was article about the opening of the Bishop Auckland and Spennymoor railway. The new line was three and a half mile long and The Edgar Memorial Band performed and was conducted by Mr J. Crawford.

In December 1886, Thomas Bramley, a workman engaged at Messrs Bolckow and Vaughans extensive collieries at Auckland Park was stabbed in the right breast in Newgate Street. A young man named Iveson, of Auckland Park was apprehended. The portal said Tom.

In August 1889, Patrick Flynn Beehouse, of the Welcome Inn, applied for a wine licence but was refused.

In the 1891 census, 25 Waldron Street isn't listed as a pub. Hannah Dunlop, aged 40 and William C. D. Feddon, aged 27 was a lodger. He was a curate of St Peters Auckland and is listed as clergy.

In the same census, the children's home was 27 and 28 Waldron Street. Robert Rutherford, who was a railway signalman, lived with wife Sarah and daughters Elizabeth and Mary. The inmates living there were Jane Stephenson, aged 12, Arnold H Bennet, aged 11, Francis R. Bennet, aged 10, Amy Jackson, aged 12, Eliza M Elliott, aged 12, Alice M Wadham, aged 12, Jane H. Wadham, aged 11, Percy G. Wadham, aged 9, Robert Alder, aged 9, Millicent L. Moor, aged 13, Martha Tallon, aged 6, Mary Humer, aged 10, Mary H. Oliver, aged 10, Albert Alderson, aged 9, Prescilla Alderson, aged 6. We had a Cilla come through the portal at Gregg Bros.

There was a bone dealer aged 77 called Thomas Wheatley who's business was in Finkle Street in 1892. The portal said Tom.

In March 1893, Mr Dobinson, a chemist, made a bid for a house known as 'south view' on Waldron Street.

In June 1893, a farewell meeting was held for Rev. Norman Macleod.

In January 1895, there was a newspaper article stating that the Orphanage founded and conducted by Mrs Lingford was to close. Was this the children's home we were picking up on?

In May 1896, the colliery offices were at 26 Waldron Street.

At Hall terrace Mary Jane, wife of William Henry Athey, late of Hebburn, aged 27 years. This was in January 1899. The Talker 2 said Mary. The portal said Bill.

There was a lady called Mary Hewitt residing in George Street that was knocked down by a bus, this was featured in 1900. The Talker 2 said Mary.

In June 1900, John Smith, of The Welcome Inn, was charged with keeping his house open during prohibited hours on a Sunday. He was fined 10s. The portal said Jack which is short for John.

In October 1900, Matthew Cunningham of Waldron Street was charged with breach of the peace.

In the 1901 census, Charles Robinson, aged 40, was the beer house keeper and fruiter, Florence Robinson, 13, daughter, John Robinson, 12, son, and Edward J. Robinson, 9, son lived at the Welcome Inn. The portal said Jack which is short for John.

In the 1911 census, Charles Robinson, aged 50 was the innkeeper. He lived with wife Ellen, aged 43, Edward Jackson Robinson, aged 19, son, Margaret Kathleen Robinson, aged 8, daughter and Albert Vincent Robinson, aged 6, son. They lived at the Welcome Inn.

In march 1911, Herbert and Samuel Moyle, brothers, were summoned for being quarrelsome and refusing to quite the Welcome Inn. Charles Robinson was the landlord and had to give evidence.

In March 1932, Mrs Lottie Elizabeth Brown was granted a decree nisi in the divorce court on the grounds of the misconduct of her husband, George Matthews Brown, miner, with a woman at Bishop Auckland. Mrs Brown admitted misconduct with a man who was willing to marry her.

In the 1939 register, William McAdam lived at the Welcome inn with Sarah M Dobbing who was the licensee. Elizabeth Dobbing also lived there and was listed as unpaid domestic duties. The portal said Bill.

In November 1939, an old man named William Stout, who lived in Waldron Street, had broken his arm and was taken into hospital. Frederick Taylor and John Thomas Lyons were charged with attempted larceny. Taylor was seen in the front room of the house and Lyons was in the back street. The back door of the house had been broken open and articles had been collected together for removal. The portal said Bill and Jack.

There was a newspaper article about Jack Morrison, a trade unionist from Percy Street Bishop Auckland. Jack took an active part in the agitation for the feeding of poor children. At the time the unemployed had to break stones for a shilling a day and 3d for each child. This was in June 1945. The portal said Jack. We also picked up on children who may have gone to a children's home.

In October 1956, George Dobinson, aged 35, of Low Waldron Street was found gassed. I picked on someone who had gassed themselves. Could it have been George?

IN THE BAR

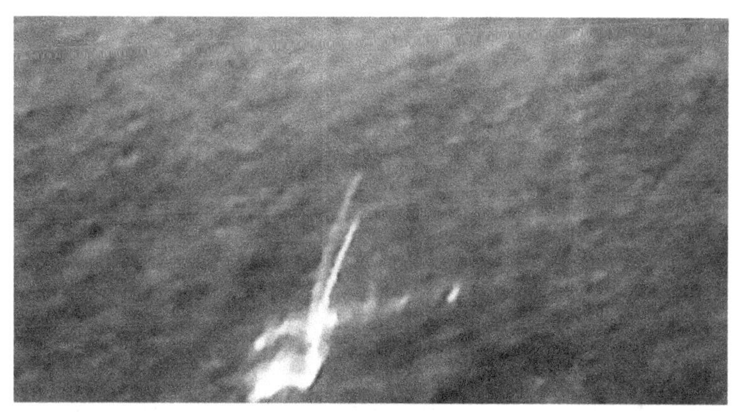

WRITING

JASMINS PHOTO OF THE DARK FIGURE.

CRE8IVE GRAPHICS

Cre8ive graphics are the suppliers of our printed hoodies, T shirts and polo tops and I got talking to a member of staff about our books. She told me that their buildings have spirits and that many people have had experiences whilst working. I asked her if she ever wanted us to investigate, we would gladly do it and include it in our 3rd book about Bishop Auckland.

Wayne (the owner) agreed to allow us access. Whilst picking up my orders I had noticed a man watching from the top of the stairs so knew that whoever was there was happy to make themselves known. We set the date and It was ages away as we were in the middle of a pandemic but it soon came around. I contacted Cre8ive Graphics to see how big the building was and got a shock when they told me the size of it. I knew then that we may have to split the investigation in 2 parts as we wouldn't be able to keep going for that long.

I also decided not to use the CCTV cameras as I wasn't keen on showing the world the stock that they hold. It just didn't seem right.

We arrived at the buildings just as a storm was due and had just gotten the equipment inside when the heavens opened. Michael gave us the guided tour and Gina was right it was huge. It was like a rabbit warren with little rooms in all directions. It was also incredibly hot and we were all sweating!

We went back into the main shop to say the prayer and grab the equipment. We carried the Handy Cam, voice recorder, Poppy bear, the new EMF bear and cameras. We made our way to the top floor.

I couldn't get my words out properly as I was talking to people and just put it down to being a long day. Shayna placed the doll that detects EMF on the floor and Carla hung behind to turn the lights off.

I asked Hannah if she was picking anything up before I started shouting out. I also asked Shayna and Bev. Shayna was picking up a brain injury and it was a man. I had a bad left leg and still couldn't say it. Shayna said that I had loss of speech and I wondered if it was the brain injury that Shayna's was picking up on.

Hannah heard a child speak when we were walking around and I asked if she was picking her up. She said she was about 4 years old. She was picking up on a man wearing a Camel coloured work coat and he worked there a number of years ago. He worked there with his brother.

I said I had a weird pain in my leg and it was at the side. Hannah wondered if it was thrombosis. She asked if it was pulling a bit and I said it was quite painful. Bev wondered if it was sciatica but it isn't because I've had sciatica and it felt different. Hannah felt that she was picking it up too and like its cutting off the blood supply.

We were all sweating cobs and I said that I was at fat club in the morning and hopefully would lose weight. I asked if they had a name. Shayna got Burt and Hannah got Robert and George. They were brothers but more twins and were close in age. As I was panning around the room with the Handy Cam I had caught a door opening on two occasions. Only wide enough for someone top peek through the first time but on the second one it opens wider and you can see a couple of children watching. I didn't realise at the time as I don't watch what I am recording.

I heard a whining sound and asked if it was Bev but it wasn't. Luckily this was caught on voice recorder but not on Handy Cam which means the child was close to the voice recorder that was on the shelf.

I turned on the portal to do a session, fumbling in the dark as it was pitch black. I said that I would turn it down so I didn't scare Gina who was working in the office.

We caught an EVP on Handy Cam saying 'there's nothing on' it was a lady.

It's coming (lady)

Thanks (lady)

Can you give us your name please?

Jack (man)

Bisden (man)

***laugh (child)**

Hi, good to talk to you.

Alma (man)

It's Jack (lady)

I changed the settings.

Hello, can you come and talk to us?

Speak (man)

Can you give us your name? is Robert here?

Mam (boy)

Hi.

Is George here? Or Robert?

Busy (lady)

Busy? Can he stop what he's doing and talk?

What about the child?

Mavis (child)

Did you say Mavis?

Yeah I did (child)

Alice (or) Howard (lady)

Who else is here?

Matthew (man)

Matthew?

Yes, Howard (man)

There's a lot of you.

What is it? (man)

What is it? I've just come to talk to you. That's all.

David (man)

David? Can you tell me what this building used to be?

The portal turned off.

What did this building used to be?

***music**

That's dramatic!

Called Abbie (man)

Who's Abbie?

Did you like your music?

Alright? (man, cockney accent)

*music

Was there a music hall here? Did you work at the hippodrome?

Michael told us that there was a pub next door.

Did you like the music?

Nancy (lady)

Ooh (lady)

Ooh?

What a finish (man)

Died (child)

Can you tell me something about this building that I don't know? Which is a lot because I don't know anything about it.

Yeah (man)

Who's the child?

Bossy (man)

We'll see?

Did you work here?

Dr Lowe (man)

Did you work here? It's lovely to talk to you.

The portal turned off.

My street (man)

Your street? Did you live here?

Did you live in the street?

Garden row (lady)

What number peel street did you live?

Bev thought it said high street.

Did you live in the high street?

Brighton (man)

Brighton?

Are you from the hippodrome? (Hannah)

That's a long way to come.

Shayna got the number 74.

Break it (lady)

Brighton? I've never been to Brighton.

Who's there? (lady)

Could be off (lady)

Could be off? Howay then let's go.

Get your stuff (man)

Lisa (lady)

Come and tell me what you used to do for a living.

I'm Fred (man)

Hannah (lady)

Did you work here? or did you work at the pub?

Bedtime (lady)

***music**

Were you a singer?

Herrington (man)

We caught an EVP on voice recorder saying 'its arthur'

Who do people see out of the corner of their eye in here?

Who is it that people see?

Tom (child)

We caught an EVP of a lady saying 'he's a pig'.

Did you say Tom?

Michael said that there's a tom that works there.

What's your name? (cockney man)

Do you mean tom who works here?

For the vet (man)

Or is your name Tom?

I never (man)

Earn it (child)

Nancy (lady)

Was that Nancy?

Who is Nancy?

From Bishop (man)

Your busy? Sorry.

You have said your busy twice now.

I'm from Trenton? (man)

In the front row?

Yes (lady)

From bishop (lady)

I'm saving (lady)

You're sick? What are you sick of? Are you poorly?

You! (lady)

Me? You're sick of me? well I'm sorry.

We have just come to learn a bit about you.

I love it (man)

Are you sick of me asking questions?

David (cockney man)

David?

Michael said that David works with him too and works with Tom.

I'm upset (cockney man)

Does David work here?

Rachel (man)

Michael said that Rachel is Wayne's wife. I have also found out since that my relation who is also called Rachel works there.

We caught a very clear EVP saying 'where Michael'.

Hannah said that they are definitely aware of who works there.

I said that is intelligent and not just a spirit that walks through walls.

Independent (lady)

Do you like how its run now?

Lydon (lady)

Do you like what its used for? Its chocker block.

Do you like what they've done to the place? (Hannah)

Yes (lady)

I bet the kids love it.

They'll explore (man)

They explore? I'm not surprised.

Do you go in the attic bit?

Attic (man)

That said attic didn't it?

Is that your favourite part?

We caught an EVP on voice recorder of a man saying 'go in to think'.

Do you want to know what my favourite part is?

The cold bit!

Your mad (man)

I like the cold bit to be fair. Is it where you used to keep the veg?

So I take it your were something to do with fruit and veg then?

I reckon (lady)

Correct (man)

What did you used to sell most? Potatoes?

Go on (man)

I like a tatie.

The weekend (lady)

The weekend? You used to sell lot of veg at the weekend?

70 (lady)

70?

Forget (lady)

Michael told us that Tommy Redfearn used to have his veg place in the building.

Enquiry (man)

He said it was about 30 years ago. I remember Tommy from when he used to do the rounds on his van

From Sid (man)

Is this Tommy Redfearn?

It could be that he's talking about tommy or it might be Tommy. (Hannah)

Murder (man)

Is Tommy Redfearn here?

Tommy (man)

Please stop (man)

Tell them (man)

Yesterday (man)

I remember Tommy from when I was little.

I.P. or Ivy (man)

***music**

Disappear (man)

Cards (man)

Racist (man)

What year was this built? Can you tell me?

It's time (lady)

How old is it? To you know?

It's close (man)

It turned it off. I'll do it once more and then we will do an EVP session.

If I put the microphone on will you talk to us?

If you knock it off I'll take it as a hint.

Sister (man)

Edmund (lady)

Who is Edmund?

I am (man)

Leave (man)

There's lots of people coming and going isn't there? Are they all from the street?

Do you want us to knock this off?

Stay In it (lady)

Are you from London?

Did you travel here? Because I don't think you are from here are you?

Were you a performer?

Ivy (lady)

Was here (man)

Hannah asked Michael if he has ever heard his name when there was no one around. He says he has heard someone shouting and has replied, only to find that there hasn't been anyone there.

Name (child)

Carla said she's heard someone whistle.

Julie (lady)

Hannah asked Michael if he was interested in working with spirit as she felt that he was quite psychic.

The portal turned off and played classical music again so we knocked it off.

Hannah was talking to Michael about spirit and how they make him aware of their presence because he wasn't scared.

Michael said he has had quite a few experiences within the building. Hannah said that there is a man who liked to be around him and he was intelligent. He knew exactly what was going on and he was there to help.

Bev took some photos and I took some too on the full spectrum.

Michael said he was a bit worried about being a target. I said that sometimes they try so very hard to talk to people and when they realise he can hear them they get excited. So Hannah explained to him how he should just acknowledge them.

I said that its best to acknowledge them because people think that if they ignore it things will stop but we have found that the opposite actually happens. Where it might have been subtle before, the more they try the more happens. So you are better off just saying that you can hear them and asking them not to scare you.

Michael asked if the spirit would follow us home tonight, I said that they shouldn't because we do a prayer and ask them not to. But I felt that the spirit knows Michael anyway because he sees him every day. He asked if this man could follow him home and I assured him that he shouldn't as his loved ones and guides wouldn't let him get that close. But it could be that the gentleman is protective of him. The gentleman must feel comfortable around them all. When we come along we like to learn about them and find out who it is. Hannah suggested saying goodnight to them as you would a work colleague. Then they know their place and you know yours.

I decided to do a couple of EVP sessions before moving on. I explained to Carla and Michael that EVP sessions were where I ask the questions, pause for a bit and hope that spirit have spoken to us. i asked Hannah if it was still Robert and George or was Tommy more prominent now.

Hannah said that the gentleman with him has been at the building from the beginning and isn't given his name. When Michael started at the business it was smaller in size so he had watched the business grow. Hannah felt that this gentleman had watched Michael grow with the business.

I said the man obviously likes the fact that Michael is comfortable with it and Michael said that it was nice to know.

I felt a cold breeze down my arm and it felt nice.

I asked if there were any spirits in the room with us could they come next to me and talk into this device?

Is there a gentleman here that's quite friendly with Michael? We just want to learn a little bit about you. We aren't here to disrespect you or anything like that. We just want to know your name really. I know the machine said Tom and Hannah picked up on a Robert and a George but we don't know if that's you. So if you could tell us that would be great.

Bev said that my watch was caught on the recordings again and I took it off.

Are there any children in this building that can come and talk to us please? We would like to know if you're here as well. We caught an EVP saying 'Abbie'. Can you come and talk into this thing that I'm holding. Then I can learn about you and find out who you are. You can tap on the microphone if you aren't keen on talking. Or you could bang on something or tap on a box.

When we listened back we heard that we had caught the EVP and thought it said Abbie. I said that we should try to find out who Abbie is.

Is your name Abbie? Did we catch you? Did you live here Abbie? Tap.

Or did your parents live here? Tap.

Do you know how old you are? Again tap on something if you like if you don't want to talk. Tap.

We have a doll over here, it's a scary doll, but you can play with it if you want. Tap. Little did we know that the doll would get moved not long after.

We decided to move on and Carla went to put the lights on. We didn't go far, just along the corridor into the next room and this was where Hannah heard the child when we had the walk around. We shouted to tell Carla to turn out the lights and we tried a portal session.

Abbie are you here?

Abbie (lady)

Abbie? What's your second name?

Anne (child)

I'm a girl (child)

I said that she was saying something but it couldn't make it out.

Abigail (man)

Abigail? That's a lovely name.

Acid (man)

Beg your pardon?

Who's Abigail?

Marlo (man)

Good job (man)

Is she your daughter?

You're kidding (lady)

Job (man)

Hello (child)

Arthur (child)

It's nice to hear from you.

Thankyou (boy)

Your welcome! What can you tell me about this place?

Did you work here?

Was it a shop? (Hannah)

Job (man)

Was it a warehouse? (Hannah)

Copied it (man)

Was there a fire close to here?

Hannah said as I said it she picked up on soot. I got the smell of a fire.

Who had a fire?

I did (lady)

Was there a fire in the street or something?

I noticed the portal was moving and it tipped back.

Hello?

Darling (man)

Is that better?

Yeah (man)

We will just leave it there then.

No (man)

Hannah said that it likes moving it lately.

Did you find it funny? You made everyone jump with it last week.

Thank you (man)

Come and tell me about you.

Marlon (man)

Let the world know.

Is Abbie with us? (Hannah)

Michael could feel a cold draught.

Who is Abbie? I'd like to know about Abbie.

The Caesar (lady)

Do you see this on the floor here?

Little Al (man)

You can go next to it and the paws will change colour. Hannah asked them to go close the REM pod and light the lights up.

You don't need to be scared of them.

Doing it (lady)

Pete (man)

You come and tell us about you. I'm going to put you in a book you know.

We are going to tell the world about you.

Ok, where's he at?(man)

At work (lady)

At work?

Yes get him to come here (man)

Are you at work?

Hannah asked if a dog came in at any time. Michael said that Wayne's dog sometimes comes in.

Hannah (man)

Hannah felt that the dog did sense things. Michael said it doesn't come very often.

Hey you (lady)

The spirits know that the dog comes in. the man and the little girl like the dog (Hannah)

Vince (man)

I like dogs.

We just feel it (lady)

I said that I had caught a bright light next to the portal. Carla said the bear was moving. She could see its arm moving.

Laughing (lady)

Are you moving the teddy bear?

The portal turned off.

I said that I freaks everyone out. That bear is called Poppy. I said that I saw the light at the same time as Carla saw the bear move.

Where would you like is to go next?

Do things get put down and not where they are put? (Hannah)

Michael said that it was hard to tell.

The portal stopped and played classical music again

Hannah felt that they moved things. Michael said they cant find things in the building. Michael said that Carla's phone disappeared years ago and hasn't been seen since.

Who's took Carla's phone? Do you know?

Her cousin (lady)

Who's your cousin?

Have they pinched it?

Yes (child)

She had put it on a shelf and disappeared. Its not been seen since and they thought a customer had pinched it.

Where the phone at? Can you tell us where it is? How about as a magic trick, tomorrow you put it somewhere where she can find it.

At her mums (lady)

You put it somewhere and that'll be brilliant. That would be a brilliant trick. It's no good to you is it? You can't phone anyone. You have to use this gadget when you like to talk.

Carla would like her phone back. Can you just put It where she can find it please? That'll be great cos she loved that phone. (Hannah)

End (man)

Which end?

We caught a child crying on Handy Cam.

***laughing (child)**

Has a child pinched it? Is it Abbie who has took it?

It stopped it and played classical music again.

Who likes classical music?

Do you like the music I play downstairs? (Michael)

Not a lot of people do (Michael)

I asked if it was a bit heavy and he said it was actually a bit cheesy.

I love cheesy music.

Do you like the cheesy music? I bet you don't even know what cheesy music is.

Do you prefer piano?

Yes (man)

Are we going to move on. Are you going to come?

I decided to try and EVP session before we moved on.

Michael that it would be the icing on the cake if the phone turned up. they said that they tried to ring it and everything but nothing. Hannah said that sometimes you have to ask them to return it.

If there are any spirits in this room that knows where Carla's mobile phone is, you probably don't know what a mobile phone is, but it's a little thing that went missing a few years ago. do you know where it is? What is Abbie that took it? Or was it stolen by a customer? There wasn't a response.

I'm just going to ask once more because through the portal you said it was your cousin that took it. Does anybody know what happened to Carla's private property that went missing? Do you know where it is?

Do you know who has got it? Will you give it back please because she wants it back its not yours? If you could give it back that would be really good. She would be really grateful. Although she won't be using it now. but that would be nice if you could return it because then she would know that you were good and kind. We did get some tap responses on the microphone.

We decided to move to the next room. We went to the main office.

I emptied out the contents of my pockets onto the large table. Bev asked if she could sit at one of the desk and an EVP was caught on Handy Cam of a man saying 'does the sun come up' and 'welcome'.

Michael asked us if we would walk around the office and see if we could sense where it felt strange. Both Hannah and I felt that it was at the desk right at the back and I felt that there was a static feeling in the doorway. Shayna said that she could hear a tapping sound where she was stood.

Michael asked if we wanted to know why he was asking and I told him to pop over and see if he could feel it. He could feel the tingling where we were. I could feel that the spirit had just stepped right up to me and Hannah felt like she had an electric shock. The energy had then moved to where Michael was stood. He told us that where energy was is the whole of the area that he worked at.

Michael pointed out where all of the people that were mentioned through the portal sat and that Wayne had an office in the next room and its where Rachel is when she visits.

I also felt that spirit would be using all of their energy and building strength. Michael said that one night it was caught on the CCTV that all of the monitors came on and went off over a series of 2 hours. You could see a ball of energy passing around each desk and the following morning it was like nothing had happened.

The room was full of equipment that would use a lot of heat and power and it was probably why they did things in that room. I felt that I had a bad headache and Hannah also felt that she had been hit on the head.

Michael said that he too suffered from a lot of headaches whilst working in that room. I said that when it happened he should ask them to back off a bit as it probably wasn't his. I felt that because he was quite sensitive anyway, spirit would put feelings on him to show what they suffered with in life. It happens all of the time on investigations.

Hannah was asking Michael about the dog and he said that it doesn't come that often. Hannah felt that the dog would whine if a certain door was closed. Michael said that when he's sat at his desk he would often hear his name shouted and when he calls back it isn't one of his work colleagues.

I told him that it would frequently happened to me and that I also would hear my front door open and close and that there wouldn't be anyone there. Carla said that she had experienced that at home too. Hannah said its common for them to mimic the voice of someone you know.

Michael said that it made sense as it was Wayne's voice he would often hear. I said that its just for attention and that it's not harmful but they probably find it funny. Michael said that was a joker at work so they were playing a joke on him and getting their own back on him. At least the spirits in the building had a sense of humour as we had come across lots of uptight spirits who had no sense of humour at all.

Hannah gave her thoughts on what happened to evil people when they died and if they didn't learn from their mistakes they are sent back to learn it again. She strongly believes in reincarnation.

We started to talk a bit about TV programmes that do what we do and that the camera was never anywhere near where something happened but I said that usually happened to us too. Michael asked if we think spirit did it intentionally and I think that is true. That's why it is better to use CCTV and try to cover every angle.

Michael said that even though Wayne wasn't interested in the investigation he would probably be watching the CCTV so I gave him a wave. Hannah said that someone in the office was a bit nervous about what happened in the building and Michael felt that it might be Gina. I said that I would have probably made things worse as I've been talking to her about it all. She said that her daughter worked there as a temp and didn't come back following the things that happened.

I decided to try a portal session but try as I might I couldn't get the portal to work!

Oliver (man)

Who is the person that likes to wander around in here with Michael?

Here (child)

Shayna picked up on Billy and Michael said that Billy worked there.

Billy? Are you naming all of the staff?

I couldn't get the portal to work properly and one of the batteries had drained. I changed the battery but it still wouldn't work.

You aren't going to talk are you? I think I'll have to change the wire

Help (lady)

Did it say help there? (Bev)

It sounded like help. What do you need help with?

David (lady)

Should I go and get a wire?

If you want (child)

If you want? Oh thanks.

I went downstairs to grab a new wire that attaches the battery.

Are you messing with my stuff?

Yes (child)

Well.

There we go its working now.

I put the old wire and battery back in and its now working.

Who was the spirit who was turning on the TV's? I know they aren't tv's but you might know them as TV's.

Can you give us your name?

Maybe you could turn them on again? (Shayna)

Hannah felt that the energy was building.

What's your name please?

Out (man)

Out? Have you had enough of us?

It's because Gina's there. (Michael)

Who's the lady next door do you know?

We caught an EVP of a lady saying 'what are you leaving for?'

Michael pointed out that his computer screen had come on. Bev went around to film it.

Who has turned the computer on? Do you know?

Shayna said that you can hear the tower working and I said that it wasn't on when we were there earlier.

Bev asked spirit if they could put the other TV's on. She also commented on how tidy his desk was and it was a pity the others weren't!

I changed the channel.

Is that better?

Am I interfering with you now?

Did you like the other one better?

No (man)

I changed the channel back. Bev sat back down and the chair went down.

Michael suggested putting it on his desk and I moved.

Are you going to talk to us over here?

I said that his desk was lovely and tidy.

Do you like it cos its tidy?

Have you gone quiet?

You're not shy are you?

Spirit just wouldn't talk through the portal so I knocked it off.

Hannah asked Michael if he felt drained in the room and he said he felt drained all of the time. But it could be because it was so hot.

I decided to do an EVP session.

Am I stood where your stood?

Did you turn the monitor on? We caught an EVP saying 'no'.

Can you give us your name please? Did you have a head injury? Or did you suffer with headaches or a blow to the head?

Hannah said someone had difficulty breathing.

Did you have difficulty breathing?

I played the recording back and said that I had gone ice cold. As I said it we caught an EVP of a man saying 'just then, just a minute'.

Little girl you know you're not going to get wrong of us. We aren't going to tell you off. Honestly, we don't mind. I thought I heard someone cough and asked if it was Gina so went to have a look but she wasn't there. An EVP was caught on Handy Cam saying 'bairns'.

Hannah said that she felt that she was stood and kept forgetting to breathe.

Michael said that the doll moved in the corner and Shayna saw it move out of the corner of her eye.

Do you like that doll? It's fairly ugly to be fair. Have you been moving that doll? Honesty you're not going to get wrong. If you want to touch the doll, you touch the doll.

I asked her to knock it off and give it a push but it wouldn't whilst we were watching. We didn't think the CCTV would reach that far and it goes back to what we were saying about doing things away from the camera.

I said that it wouldn't do anything now as we were watching and they don't work that way. Our best chance would be to leave it in view of the camera and walk away.

I never saw you mind, but I'm impressed.

Hannah wondered if it was Abbie.

Do you like that dolly? She could do with a hairbrush.

Shayna said that she tried to brush it earlier.

Were you trying to brush her hair?

I said that we had had some quite impressive interaction in the room. The screen came on, we had caught EVPs and the doll moved on its own.

I went to stand near the doorway and said that someone definitely had a problem with their head. I asked spirit if they had fallen or something. I also said that I was getting confused and had trouble putting my words together too.

Is there anybody here that suffered with forgetfulness? Did you have a bad memory? Did you usually forget what you were going to say? Or maybe you fell? Maybe you went dizzy, lost your footing and fell? And who is the person who moved the dodgy doll in the corner? Was that Abbie? We caught an EVP on Handy Cam saying 'yes'.

I asked the team if they wanted to move on. Shayna asked if we were leaving the doll there and I suggested moving it so that it could be picked up on CCTV if it moved. Shayna said she only placed in front of the cupboard because there was a tapping sound coming from there earlier.

I told spirit that we were going to move the dolly for them. Shayna moved it and placed it on a desk and banged really hard on the desk just to make sure it didn't move easily. Michael showed us a clown that they had that when it wobbled on the rounded bottom it has a bell that made a noise. Michael said that sometimes it makes the noise on its own.

Hannah felt that someone in the building had seen something but won't admit to it. We asked where we should investigate next. Carla reckoned in the shop as people have seen things and Michael said in Wayne's office because people who live in the flat next door say they have seen something and they were wondering if the building was one large one and it goes through from one to the other.

Michael said that when was is in this room and stood at the desk has often seen things out of the corner of his eye. He also said people get the feeling of being watched. I told Gina to just ignore us and Michael could see Wayne on the CCTV camera. He was stood outside.

I asked Hannah if she was picking anything up in the office and Hannah felt there was a smaller man. Wayne joined us in his office but I could tell he was quite sceptic. We caught a light anomaly on the Handy Cam travelling down the screen.

Hannah was talking about the gentleman and that he was strict. I asked Hannah if he would talk to me if I put the portal on.

Are you going to talk to me please?

The boss man's here now.

Is he? (man)

Yeah he's come to make sure everything's ok and his workers are still working.

Who's the little man? I know you don't like being called that. Who is the shorter gentleman?

Arthur (lady)

***music**

Is Abbie still here?

??

I thought it had seemed to have died off and had pulled away. They had being going for 2 hours.

Are you sick of us?

Shayna still felt like she had a weird feeling at the front of her right leg.

It's very quiet.

Do you want us to go home and leave you in peace?

We caught a heavy breath on Handy Cam like someone couldn't breathe.

And that's what happens! They just go.

Nothing was coming through the portal at all. I said that they had maybe called time.

I asked if they would say goodbye to us before we go.

Gaynor (lady)

It knocked it off at number 999 on the portal.

I get the feeling you are sick of us. Bev wanted us to have a break and try again but I felt the spirits had gone. I said that we could still have a break and try downstairs but I felt that it had gone from this room.

Shayna asked if she should grab the doll and I said it hadn't given much time to move it. We caught an EVP of a man saying 'yes'. Michael and Carla told Wayne about what had happened to the room but looking at the monitor it didn't look like it would have been caught on CCTV.

We made our way downstairs into the shop and Michael told us that this was apparently where they used to fix trucks and stuff that collected stuff from the railways. There is also meant to be fuel tanks under the floors somewhere. I asked if there was fire sometime but he didn't know. The Moore's owned this building and Tommy Redfearn rented it from them. Michael said that when he first started working for the company it was all open plan, and they had knocked through what was an archway and made the building bigger.

It was time to investigate the final part of the building and Hannah tried her Echovox.

It said 'help. Jack, he's come, hi'.

I asked them to come and talk to us, even though they would be sick of us. We were all tired and had worked really hard.

'Jump, Jack, Anne, you, listen, Jack'.

Bev was moving in the shop and made me jump.

I went to take some photos. Shayna said that something was touching her arm and I was getting a chest pain. She felt that something was wrong with her arm and leg. She kept hearing movement too. Michael said that it was really cold there too.

'Listen'

Do you want us to listen?

'Prison, prison'

I asked who has been to prison and it said 'him, Jim'.

Michael said there are 2 Jim's that work there.

'Catholic'

Did you live here? 'apartment'.

Who's Ray?

I had Shayna's funny leg now and a bad head. Shayna said he must have had a limp. And Shayna felt that a person had a leg and was getting the name Ray.

Michael and Shayna were both hearing clicking and I could be someone going upstairs.

The Echovox said 'don't'.

'Ray'.

I asked them to stamp their feet as the print room was above us. something tapped on the Handy Cam.

'He's coming'. We could hear movement upstairs above us. I asked if they could stamp their feet.

'Hello'

I could feel cold around my bum like it was child height. Michael could feel cold right up to his chest.

Can you give us your name?

'Mark, Bill'

I have relations called Mark and Bill, as does Rachel that works there (as we are related).

I asked if I was anywhere near them and it replied 'yes'. I started to get a bad head again.

Have you got a bad head?

'First, Arthur'.

We went into the small room. Shayna and Bev stayed in the shop and did mirror scrying.

I shouted and asked Bev to join us in the room. I grabbed the portal and we made our way to the cold room at the back. I asked Hannah if she was getting anything and if I should bring the portal in.

I went to get the portal and turned it on but there wasn't anything coming through it. We caught an EVP on voice recorder saying 'there it is'.

What would you like to say before we go? We caught an EVP saying 'step back'.

Shayna felt lightheaded in this room.

We are going to leave you, you know?

An orb passed by the Handy Cam.

Hannah was given the name Lily and it sounded like a child. I asked about Lily and how it was a pretty name.

She said that when I went to get the portal she said no.

Michael was cold where he was stood and could feel a tingling sensation. I gave up with the portal.

I tried an EVP session.

Is there anybody in this room called Lily?

Lily we mean you no harm at all? Who's is the person who seems to have been walking around upstairs? Can you give us your name please? We didn't get a response.

I felt that someone still had a problem with their head and Shayna said someone was tickling her head.

Hannah felt that whoever it was is all over the building not in one place and liked to follow Michael. I asked her if he had a bad stomach as I was getting a stomach ache. Michael said that he suffered from bad stomach aches when at work. I was still struggling to get my words out and Hannah said that it seemed more like a migraine.

Hannah feels that he just worked through it and was a grafter. He wouldn't take a day off. Michael felt that someone was in the shop and I invited him in.

Did you have a problem with your head and your speech? Bev also felt that there was someone hovering as she could see it.

Is there someone outside in the shop while we are in here? Can you shout hello? Come and let your presence be known we mean you no harm. You can use all of our energy to show yourself to us. if you don't want to show yourself you can knock on something.

Hannah was picking up 1920 and a stiff collar.

Were you here in 1920? We caught a groaning and a breath on voice recorder.

Hannah said he had a pencil moustache and centre parting.

Did you have a little moustache? And a centre parting in your hair? I bet you looked spiffing. Can you come in here? You are welcome honestly, we don't mind it's your place not ours.

Hannah felt that he had something to do with a car. I asked if we should call it a night. And Michael reminded Shayna to pick up her doll and I asked her to take a camera with her in case it had moved but it hadn't.

The energy had dropped in the building and we decided to call it a night and end the investigation. We made arrangements to go back as we felt that there was more to discover but they weren't ready to tell us anymore information that night.

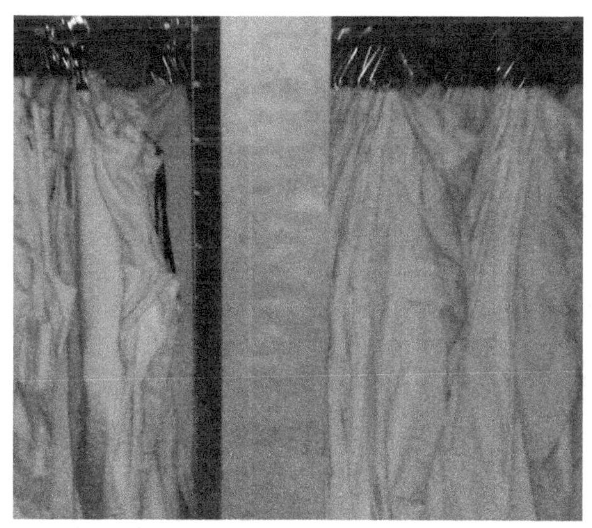

DOWNSTAIRS IN THE SHOP

IN THE SHOP

DOWNSTAIRS

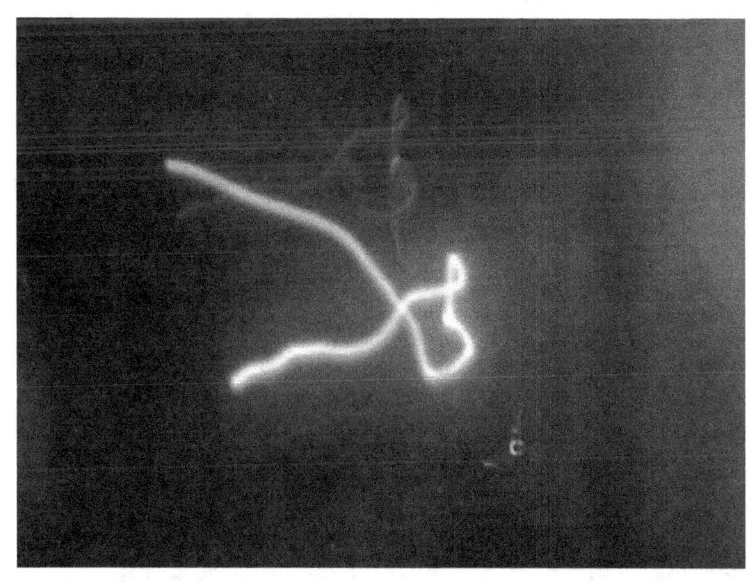

SPIRIT LIGHTS

SPIRIT LIGHTS

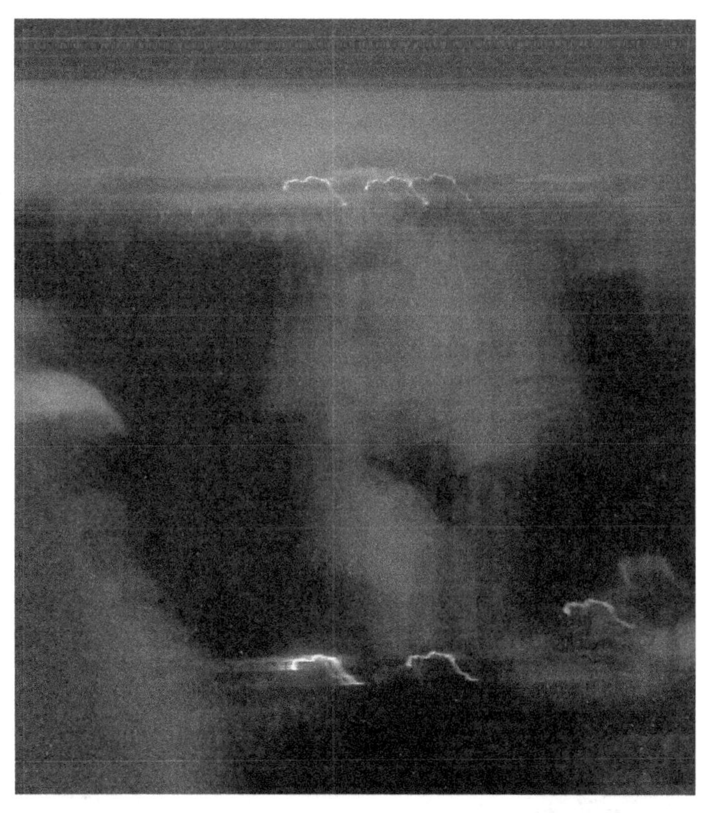

LIGHTS AND A DARK FIGURE TO THE RIGHT

FIGURES WATCHING

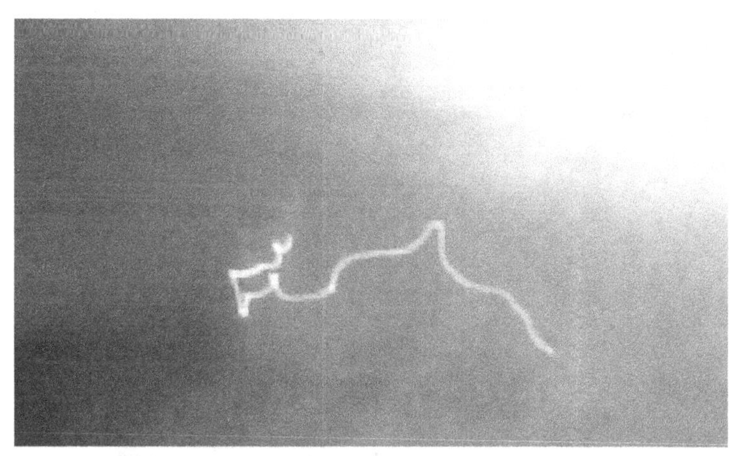

A FACE AND WRITING

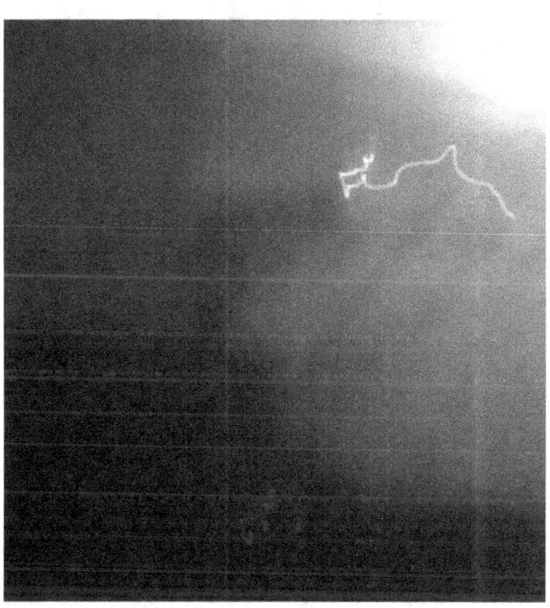

A FIGURE

FIGURES WATCHING

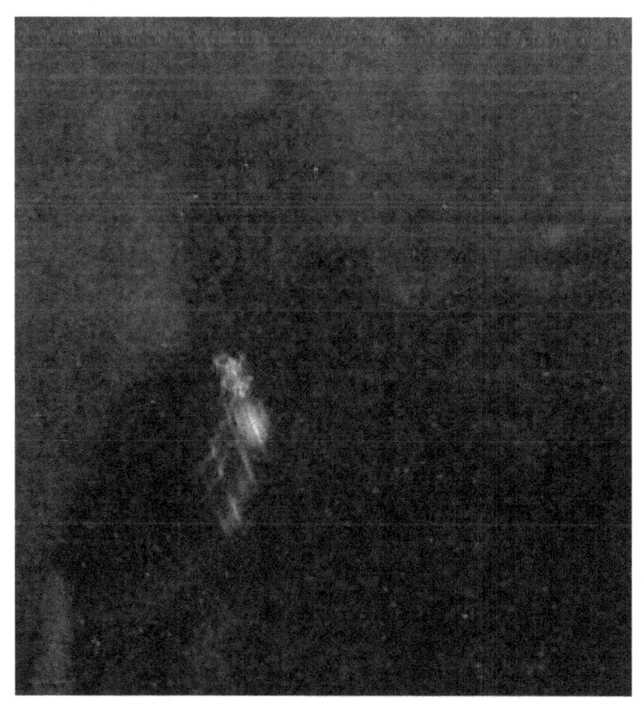

MYSTERIOUS LIGHTS

CRE8IVE PART 2

When we set up the CCTV cameras both Hannah and I heard a man's voice. It was like a muttering and it was in the embroidery room. We both thought it was Wayne and that he was still in the building but he wasn't.

Also when we were setting up CCTV the camera in Gina's room was moved and there was interference on the cables and the ball moved on its own but we weren't yet recording. Hannah was talking about a little boy being in the room.

Bev said that we love our little toys and a child's voice was caught on voice recorder. It sounded very little like a toddler saying 'Arthur'.

We sorted the portal out before carrying into the office. We couldn't find the prayer and it looked like it was in the box downstairs. Hannah went downstairs on her own to get it. Michael asked us how the research had gone from the last investigation but I honestly couldn't remember much about what I had found but it had been the summer.

Hannah returned and said that there was definitely movement downstairs when she was there. We did the prayer of protection and started the investigation.

I turned on the portal to see if the settings need changing.

Can you just let me know it's working? We've come to talk to you.

Yes (man)

Its better than (lady)

Alan (man)

Dead (boy)

Can you give us your name please?

Arthur (man)

Arthur (lady)

***whistle**

Who's whistling at me? Did you whistle at me?

I'm just getting your settings right before we move into the spooky room.

Is Abbie here?

***whistle**

It's whistling at me isn't it?

Where's Abbie?

Outside? It's no good outside its freezing.

There was a loud thud upstairs.

Stephen (man)

There was something caught on camera 4 just above us.

We're going to go into the office where you moved the camera.

We're going to hope you move it again. As we were talking a bright light appeared on the monitor.

We heard a bang and I got earache in my left ear. Hannah had it too.

Who has earache?

That's him (child)

We got music hear last time, because we said it could be from the pub.

Owen (man)

Hello, did that say Owen?

Hello.

Where it happened (man)

Have we spoken before?

Fran (lady)

Fran? Or Frank?

Are you from the area?

The attic (lady

Yes (man)

Is there a gentleman here who wears a top hat?

The portal turned off. I tried another channel.

Philip (man)

Leave them (man)

Hello.

The portal sounded like railway tracks.

Prison, track (lady)

Did you work at the railway?

Boy (lady)

Didn't do it (man)

Prison (man)

He's off (man)

Phil (man)

It's our Kevin (man)

What are you trying to tell us?

Philip (man)

That doesn't sound very nice no swearing.

I'll try to get you clearer.

Born in France (man)

I changed the channel again.

I'm here (lady)

Owen (man)

Owen? That's twice we got Owen.

Did we get Owen last time?

I know it was at Hartlepool.

Owen have we met before?

Bless you (man)

Bossy? I'm not bossy I'm just asking?

Have we met before?

Who's the gentleman with the top hat? (Hannah)

Should we go in that other room?

Agnes (lady)

I keep seeing lights, should we go in?

Boring (man)

We're coming in, I'm going to carry you and let you talk.

Cute (man)

Right we are coming in. We're going to come and see you.

Don't mind us we are just coming in.

Michael could see something on the CCTV from the other unit.

The portal went quiet.

Albert (lady)

Alistair? That was very clear?

Alistair. Is Alistair the man that wears the top hat.

Michael said that he was feeling very cold.

Well Alistair?

I could feel something behind me and Michael asked if it was cold but it was static. Hannah could feel it behind her too and she was stood next to me.

I could even feel it on my hair.

Is Alistair here? I feel like I shouldn't be calling you Alistair and that I should be calling you Mr something.

Bev said that she had caught a light anomaly on the Handy Cam.

Is there anybody here that would like to talk to us?

The portal didn't seem to be picking anything up.

We could hear voices but Michael said that it would be next door.

 I picked up on a bad wrist and wondered if it was mine. It was aching and my neck felt achy too. Hannah said her neck was heavy but she had eye strain and felt that a man was wearing a monocle. We had caught an EVP saying 'eyes' on the voice recorder.

I was also picking up on a slavery mouth, as per usual.

Have you got anything else to say? It was really clear when you said Alistair.

The portal went off.

I was seeing something behind Bev on the thermal imaging camera. It was coming and going, getting darker then lighter. It wasn't a shadow. It looked like a man wearing a top hat.

I turned the portal back on.

Michael asked if it was the man that he frequently saw in the doorway looking in. Hannah said he could be. Michael said that he often saw him out of the corner of his eye. Hannah felt that he liked to make himself known to Michael as he reminded him of someone he knew.

The battery now went on the voice recorder and I had to go for more batteries. They were definitely building up to something.

Hannah felt that the man who she was picking up liked to shout and was very vocal.

Burt (man)

Hello.

Hannah said that the lads were a good set but there was a couple of members of staff that he's not keen on.

Michael wondered if it was the man that he sees in the doorway looking through. Hannah said he was about 5ft 6".

Albert (man)

Michael said that he sees someone looking out of the corner of his eye but hasn't seen him full on.

It's me (man)

Hannah said that he was there a lot and that he likes Michael the most.

Dennis (or) devil (man)

Devil or Del? I'm hoping you said Del.

Hannah said that Michael reminded him of someone he knew when he was alive.

Jim (man)

Hannah said there was a couple he wasn't keen on and felt that I was because of the way that they acted.

Bev caught a face in a photo on her camera.

I went into the other room to get a new battery for the voice recorder.

Go back in (man)

The tried to debunk Bev's photo but couldn't.

Careful (child)

There was an EVP of a man but we couldn't make out what it said.

The others could all feel cold in the room and Hannah saw energy in the room.

Here (man)

I came back and thought that the portal had sworn.

Be angry (man)

Come and tell me something that I don't know. Can you? We've come to learn about you.

Can you tell me something about this building and next door.

Orchid (man)

Hannah said that she was given the name Paul but didn't know why. Michael said that he was linked to the building but wasn't now.

Careful (man)

Well? (man)

Well? Is that you face that is on the camera?

Hannah was given the name Eileen but didn't know if it was connect to Paul. Or Irene, she wasn't sure.

Is you name Eileen?

Anne (lady)

You were getting Percy but have you moved on from him?

Hannah said that she wasn't sure if Percy was his name or because he liked plants. They were showing her Percy Thrower. We caught an EVP of a man saying 'me'.

She said he was about 5ft 6" in height. He looked late 60s early 70s. He was a very caring bloke and had a happy nature. But he was lonely. The battery went flat on the portal. She felt that he didn't have many friends or family. I went off to get a battery.

She said that this time of year was difficult for him and she wasn't sure if he meant Christmas. She asked him to verify. He lost somebody about this time (November). It was in the 1960's but late on. He's in spirit now too though.

She felt that he could be heard in the building, like people were getting shouted at. Michael and Ross said they both do. Hannah said that it was this man and that he tries to get their attention. Michael asked the reason and she felt that he was just lonely. But he did like to play tricks and he was funny but he also had a sad side. She said to just acknowledge him, she said he thinks they are a good set of lads apart from a couple.

Arthur (man)

Arthur?

Hannah thought we got Arthur before.

Is there a Percy?

Did you have a garden? (Hannah)

He had a fruit and veg shop but he liked to grow his own veg. (Hannah)

Bernard (man)

That was why she was getting the Percy. She tried to get his name as it wasn't Percy.

Did you have a fruit and veg shop in Bishop?

I know this was fruit and veg cos I remember off before.

Purple (man)

Did you have your own shop?

Arthur (man)

Oliver?

Mark (man)

I asked if she was sure it wasn't Arthur as the portal kept saying it. She said that his name did start with A but was still asking.

She was asking if it was Andrew but couldn't quite get it.

Is it Arthur?

The portal turned off.

Did you grown veg Arthur?

Hannah asked him to show him someone she knew with the same name.

I did it (man)

It was Arthur as he showed her uncle Arthur as a reference.

I said that I loved a bit of home grown veg.

David (man)

Hannah explained that spirit use a person that she knows to let her know their name and if she didn't know anyone with that name they would show a TV personality.

I said that when she said Percy I saw my uncles face and he was called Pep.

I had a bad headache coming on and so did Hannah. She felt that he died with a stroke condition and that it went down her left side. I said that it was probably why I had a slavery mouth.

I asked him if he passed with a stroke condition.

Arthur (lady)

Yep (man)

I asked if he was disabled after it.

Yes, Arthur (man)

We ended the session to do EVPs.

If there are any spirits in the room that would like to come and communicate, can you please speak into this microphone I'm holding? Can you give me your name please? There were two taps but we realised it was the floorboards.

Sorry Arthur back to you. If this is you Arthur and you had your fruit and veg shop can you please let us know that you are here?

Is there a gentleman here that wears a top hat? EVP I think so. Do you walk through the wall to next door? I don't mean you any harm we just want to know that your there and who you are.

Do you like going to the theatre? (Hannah)

I do and its pretty local isn't it, or it was. So it was around that time then, the theatre was there. He would have been spoiled for choice in Bishop Auckland as the Eden theatre was there too. I like to go to the theatre.

Can you tell me who touched Bev's leg. We caught an EVP saying 'Amanda'. Did it feel like a lady or a man or could you not tell. She said that it just stroked her on the top of her leg.

Who stroked Bev's leg can you tell me? She said it wasn't saucy or anything like that. We caught a child's voice. I said I didn't say it was.

She might have been comforting you, I think it was a lady as I said she. Was it a lady?

We think we might have caught you saying Amanda. Is this a message for a Amanda?

Or is it a message for Bev to give her a call? (Hannah)

So is this a message for Amanda who is related to Bev. I saw a shadow in the room.

Ross started to have a coughing fit and had to leave the room for a while.

We talked for a while about Bev's relation called Amanda and that she should maybe give her a call to check on her.

It was time to move on and go downstairs so we gather up our equipment and descended the staircase and as we did something touched the top of Bev's head.

Michael told us how gets freaked out when he puts the lights on. Spirit seemed to mimic him on the Handy Cam. Hannah heard it at the time too. This moan was caught on Handy Cam but not on voice recorder. We also caught a child's voice on the voice recorder but not on the Handy Cam.

We entered the room where we had heard a man moaning earlier.

I tried a portal session.

You (man)

That's them (lady)

With bitches (man)

We thought we saw something looking around the door. It was something tall.

White (man)

Hello.

Good (man)

Hello.

Get (man)

Can you tell me who Amanda is?

Amanda (lady)

Who's Amanda?

Is it a relation of Bev's?

Adam (man)

Ted (lady)

She's a strong (lady)

Bitch (lady)

I went to take a photo of the staircase. Asking for permission as I was doing it.

No (man)

He said no. (Bev)

No? I'm here now.

I feel sick (man)

Hannah told Michael and Ross that's definitely a tinker downstairs. He liked to play tricks.

Bob (man)

Arthur Phillip (man)

Philip (lady)

I was getting a pain in my shoulder at the bottom of the stairs.

Its flop (lady)

Bev had the same pain.

Who's got a bad shoulder?

Hannah asked if the machines in the room go funny sometimes and Michael said that they do.

Burt, tap (lady)

I commented on the amount of machines in the room.

Do his tops (man)

Michael said that its where our tops would be made. Someone said it before him!

Mine as well (man)

I said mine weren't expensive ones with stitching, mine were print.

Way up (Scottish man)

Hannah said the man in the room likes to move the buttons and mess around.

She was getting the name Ernest.

Ernest?

Please (man)

Hannah said that he is a bit of a tinker.

I play tricks (man)

Yes (man)

I asked if he was a man that used to take things to bits and build them again because I was shown my father in law who liked to do the same.

Hannah said he did the same and would always have bits left over and no idea where they came from. Hannah said that he liked to mess with the dials on the machinery and he made noises to scare people.

I asked if he had an aneurism but Hannah wasn't sure. She did have a bad head but wasn't sure if he had fallen.

Are we talking about you Ernie?

Hannah also said that he likes to move things. People put things down and they would vanish.

Ernie, you sound like a bugger!

The portal went off.

Hannah said that he liked the room because of the energy. The machines gave him power and made him strong. As we were talking about it there was a thud from upstairs where we were earlier.

Hannah felt that he liked to make himself known all over the building.

Ernie is that you?

I guessed that was why my batteries were draining.

How come we didn't meet last time? Is it because we didn't come in here?

We caught an EVP on Handy Cam saying 'its Arthur'.

The portal wasn't responding.

Hannah said that he didn't like her talking about him. He liked to frighten people.

I said that he hadn't to frighten people.

She said the he was quite tall but wasn't showing what he looked like.

How am I meant to find you if you would let anyone know what you look like? She didn't feel that he was very pleasant when he was on the earth plane, he was grumpy.

I said that he needed to stop picking on people and pick on people his own size. Hannah said he laughed and on Handy Cam we caught an man saying 'bitches'.

There was a thud in another room. I felt that the table vibrated.

Michael said the he kept getting cold draughts in his face. We decided to move on.

We moved into the main shop, and went through into what was once a fridge. It still had the original heavy door and it was freezing inside. We were grateful of the cold last time as it was summer.

I asked if anyone was aware of spirit in there. I saw a butcher and Hannah saw someone with an apron on. I saw an apron with blood on it but it wasn't a butchers.

I called out and asked if they were a butcher there. I saw a leather apron and wondered who would have a Brown leather apron on. I wondered if it was a farrier and Bev wondered if he was maybe a blacksmith. We also wondered if it was Wilsons forge.

Hannah was getting touched on her shoulders. I asked if they worked at the forge.

Michael said that the buildings were houses once and that they might have been for the forge. I started to get a headache.

I did an EVP session.

If there's anybody here with us can you please tell me or let me know why I'm seeing a leather apron? Did you work at the foundry? Or Wilson's forge?

Hannah was seeing a slaughter house. As she was telling me I heard a beep like something had ran out of battery but it wasn't the Handy Cam. Hannah was seeing like a slaughterhouse in the back yard close by.

Bev said that all of the houses in the area had big back yards. Hannah was feeling a bit sick as she was experiencing it all, including the smells.

Did you have your own slaughter house? I said that there was probably a butchers at the top of the street. Bev said that it could be Gregory's.

Michael said that Lawsons butchers was close-by. Hannah also said that there were pubs too that were houses. Hannah was confused by the way that they were showing her, they weren't just houses they were other things.

We turned on the portal.

Are you a butcher?

Ian (man)

Ian or here?

Ian (lady)

Ian. Ian were you a butcher?

Yes (man)

Did you have a slaughter house?

Eva (man)

He buys them (man)

Did you have a butchers close by?

Shop (man)

Hannah was talking about a WW1 soldier with shell shock. She didn't know why she was being shown him or how he linked.

Were you a soldier?

Gun (man)

Bishop (man)

Did you go off to war?

Us (man)

Hannah could see him banging his head to try to stop hearing the awful noises.

I had a bad stomach and Hannah felt sick.

Did you live in peel street?

Go on (man)

Bobby (lady)

Bottom? Did you leave near south church road?

Price (man)

Pete (man)

I never expected you to work in here to be fair. (I was talking about the portal).

***music**

Leave (man)

I'm a bit warmer now. It must be with all of these bodies in the room.

Billy (lady)

You know we haven't got much longer. Some of us haven't been home from work yet. Infact, all of us haven't been home from work yet.

Wayne (or) Quinn (lady)

Wayne? Have you got a message for Wayne? Now's your time.

Hannah asked if any of the ladies had had their hair pulled. Michael didn't know of any and nothing came to mind.

I felt like I had headlice.

What's your message for Wayne?

Michael hoped it would be for a pay rise. And Hannah said that when she was talking to the lovely gentleman earlier he thought that they all needed their pay upping.

Does he need to give them all a bonus or something for Christmas?

Michael said we were welcome to discuss it with Wayne but he wouldn't believe us.

Do they deserve a pay rise?

Bob (man)

I think that said Bob.

Cat (man)

Who's Bob?

I was thinking, and I'm probably way off the mark here, but this is close to the Hippodrome isn't it? Signor Pepi used to wear a top hat. I wondered if there was some kind of accommodation around that he would have stayed. Michael said that next door was a pub but didn't know if it was a hotel.

He had dark hair and a top hat.

Prison (man)

I'm going to ask you. The man that wears the top hat is it Mr Pepi?

Hannah said that the man she saw in her mind's eye was very well dressed.

Is it Signor Pepi?

Yes (man)

Is Mr Pepi here?

He built the Hippodrome theatre.

Si (man)

Si? You can't talk to me like that.

I think we have met before when we did the Hippodrome, have we not?

Signor Pepi, did you stay here?

Could it not have been the Cumberland Arms? (Bev)

Yes (man)

Did you stay at the Vulcan?

Yes (man)

I just felt a breeze in my face.

It would be lovely if it was you. It might not be you, there would be lots of well to do gentlemen in Bishop Auckland, it just popped into my head.

Pat (lady)

I know you had a dog, didn't you?

Jeffrey (man)

A little King Charles or something.

Well, whoever it is in your lovely top hat, we would love to know who you are.

Hi (lady)

Well, should we knock it off.

We are going to knock you off. Thanks for talking to me.

Murder (lady)

Think (man)

I turned it off. We made our way out of the room and I closed the door behind us.

I asked if anyone was picking anything else up before we headed back up.

Hannah was aware of a child. Michael found a photo of the Vulcan and showed us where the building was. He told us that it was once the Rugby Club and owned by John Moore. He also said that John Moore owned the building we were in and that's when it because fruit and veg.

We thought we would try table tipping before heading up and Hannah heard talking so we went to try it where the voices were. We didn't have any chairs so had to do it standing.

I asked that if there were any spirit with us that they could move the table. I asked if the butcher was there. I said that I couldn't stand like that for long.

Is Mr Pepi here? The table started to vibrate. We also caught a light on camera.

I asked if there were any children there and that we just wanted to learn about them.

I asked them to move the table towards Bev and asked if the person was there that touched Bev earlier.

Bev asked them to move the table to Hannah, and I said it was their time to prove that they were there. It did move slightly. I was getting tingles underneath my hands and the table moved slightly. My back was started to hurt so we packed in. We thought we would try the table upstairs before we ended the investigation.

As we were climbing the stairs we caught an EVP of a man saying 'we're here and there' on Handy Cam.

Ross found the clown that we looked at last time and I recorded the sound on voice recorder so I could use it for our videos. Bev and Michael sat and attempted table tipping but it wouldn't work. There was a light caught on CCTV at the same time and it did dip down between them. I decided to take over from Michael and we couldn't get the table to move either. It seemed like the spirits of the building had ran out of energy, as had we, so we decided to pack everything up and finish the investigation. This investigation had been totally different to the first one. I believe that the building is like an onion, made up of many layers, all of which have their own story to tell.

SPIRIT FACES

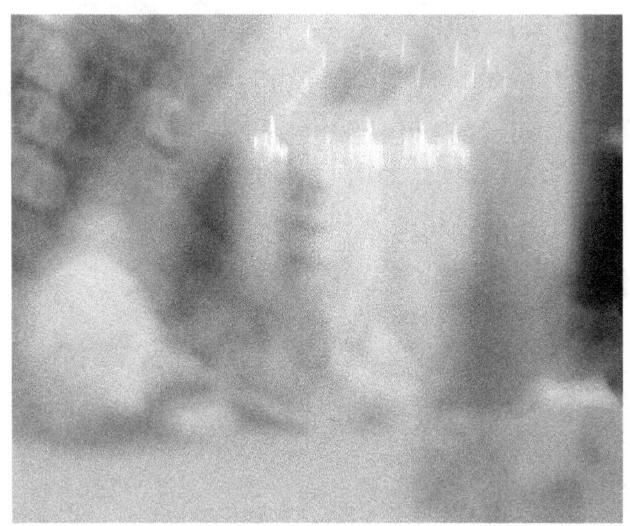

BEING WATCHED

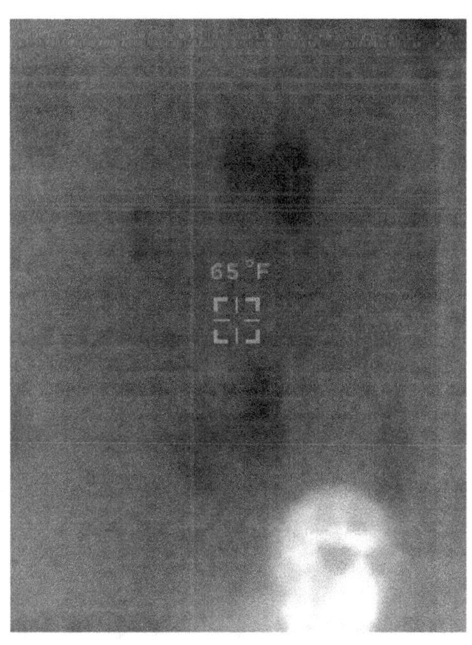

CAUGHT ON THERMAL IMAGING CAMERA

A DARK FIGURE BEHIND BEV

In December 1742, Mr Timothy Norton, late of Bishop Auckland, Apothecary deceased, left his trust to Anne Jepson, his then intended wife. His wife Anne and her children were left goods land that spread as far as Great Aycliffe.

In 1860, a young carpenter called Thomas Manners established a company and in 1868 built a new joinery workshop in Peel Street. Thomas had three sons, Thomas, George and Robert and they all worked for the company until the outbreak of the First World War when Robert enlisted in the Royal Arm Service Corps. The company contributed to the war effort by building the wings for the Sopwith Camel fighter aircraft. Hannah was aware of Thomas, George and Robert.

In November 1860, Bernard McCain died at the age of 32.

In February 1867, the recent sale of the new and commodious works near the Railway station, built for Dodds patent metal goods company, under the name of Gaunless works Company, had led to the establishment of new Ironworks at Bishop Auckland. The establishment had fallen into the hands of Joseph Vaughan and Co. The company, in addition to their present premises for casting and forging, purpose erecting rolling mills and puddling furnaces, and when the works were in full operation it was estimated employ upwards of 600 hands. The name was to be Bishop Auckland Iron Works.

In June 1875, Caroline King, wife of Francis King, metal dealer, was remanded at Bishop Auckland Police Court, by Mr H. Chaytor, charged with stabbing Agnes Weir, in North Bondgate, She accused Mrs Weir of being over familiar with her husband. After blows between then, King took a knife off the table and stabbed in the face in three places. The portal said Frank and Agnes.

In July 1878, a man names Strachan had a narrow escape from drowning in a large pond near the Iron Works. He had undressed in a public street and rolled down the embankment into the water, which was very deep. After diving into the water, which must have been almost putrid with the carcases of the innumerable dogs and cats that had drowned in it, he commenced to swim across, he began to struggle in the water. He clutched at some long grass until he regained the strength to climb out.

In November 1878, there was an article about making a roadway in peel street and it was stated that the railing of the pond had already been carried out.

In January 1880, a six inch water main was agreed to be laid from Newgate Street to Peel Street.

In March 1880, there were complaints made about the state of Peel street and no one would take responsibility as the Ironworks had been started.

In 1881, Arthur Campbell, John Craddock, Mark Raybould, George Blinton and John Horton worked at the Ironworks. The portal said Arthur, Jack (nickname for John), Mark and

Hannah picked up on George. There was also James Witcherley that worked there and the Echovox said Jim. The portal kept saying Arthur on our 2nd investigation. It also said Jim.

In June 1881, three boys picked up on clothing on the bank of the large pond belonging to the Iron Works. There was a note there too address to Mary and it was from John Jackson. The portal said Jack. It was common for people called John to get nicknamed Jack.

In December 1881, a meeting was held about the liquidation of Mr Edward Hutchinson of the Auckland Ironworks.

In January 1883, there was a dispute about the suppression of the cinder heap nuisance.

In March 1883, a conflagration of almost unexplainable magnitude in Bishop Auckland broke out and resulted in the complete destruction of the premises of Mr Thomas Manners, and extensive builder and contractor, whose sawmill and joiners shop, stocked with flammable timber, fell a ready prey to the flames, over which the utmost exertions of the Local Board Fire Brigade could obtain no ascendancy. The doomed premises extended through from Peel Street to Chester Street. Flames were observed by Mr T Pickering. The business close by were Mr J. H. Watson, also a contractor, and Messrs J & W Gibson, Wheelwrights. Mr Reeds private academy, and a store beneath, belonging Miss Scrafton, milliner on one side and Mr Mascall's premises and the Salvation Barracks on the other. The portal said Tom.

In June 1888, whilst tipping into the Ironworks pond, Peel Street, a Local Board horse backed into the water and with the cart immediately sank from view.

In November 1888, the Ironworks was up for auction. It included the land, buildings and plant.

In the 1891 census, Arthur Phillip lived at Tudhoe, Spennymoor and was a puddler. A puddler was an Iron Puddler in the occupation of Iron manufacturing. Could it be our Arthur Phillip that came through on the 2nd investigation?

In May 1891, a young man named William Atkinson, aged 21, threw himself into an old disused pond near the ironworks. It was witness by numerous people. Grappling irons were obtained but when the man was brought to the surface he was dead. The deceased worked at Brokenback Colliery and he left his brother Frank whilst walking home. The portal said Bill and Shayna picked up on Bill too. The portal said Fran or Frank on the 2nd investigation.

The inquest was carried out at The Green Tree Inn and it was discovered that William and Frank had been drinking in the Mitre Pub but had started to fight on the way home. Another witness Mrs Robertson had said that he had called at her house and said that he was going to his mother. He was told his mother was down the street, to which he replied not that mother, my real mother. He then said you will never see me again. One witness said that there was a fearful smell from the pond especially when the water was disturbed. There was no protection to anyone, especially on a foggy night. A juryman said that pigs which had swine flu had been pulled out of the pond. The jury had an opinion that it was a wonder that the stench pool in the centre of town hadn't caused a serious illness. The portal said Fran or Frank on the 2nd investigation.

In June 1891, following the recent suicide, the local board considered the question of Peel Street Dam. They discussed the use of quicklime, how to fill the pond and filter the water away. The dam was deemed as a disgrace and that the smell from it would knock someone over.

In April 1892, there was a fire at the site of the old Ironworks. Mr William Hudson, wood merchant, was completely gutted. The portal said Bill and Shayna picked up on Bill too.

In July 1892, John Cant was charged by P.C. Coyne with committing a breach of the peace because of fighting at Peel Street. The defendant pleaded guilty.

In August 1898, a journalist called John Abbey died suddenly from heart failure. He was aged 51 and left a widow and 5 children. Was this why the portal said Abbie? Was it referring to this man and not a girl?

In the 1901 census, there is a Lily Beaston, aged 17, was a servant at Victoria Crescent. Hannah picked up on a Lily and the portal said Bisdon. Was it Beaston?

In the 1901 census, Amanda Stoddart lived at St Andrews Terrace. Was this the Amanda we were aware of on our 2nd visit.

In 1904, there was an auctioneers called C. H. Hutchinson at Peel Street. They were selling plants, trees and shrubs.

In July 1908, there was a sad cycling accident happened on the last lap of the race on the corner of the grammar school. Thomas Masean Ipsen, aged 25, had been pushed from his bike and suffered a head injury. The died from internal haemorrhage, causing compression of the brain. Arthur Creasor Swales, a fruiterer from Bishop Auckland was an umpire that day. Was this the Arthur that came through on the 2nd investigator. Was this why I felt a brain aneurism and forgetfulness?

In September 1909, William Fullock, landlord of the Vulcan Hotel and Thomas Thompson, cartman both drowned whilst swimming at Tynemouth whilst on a day trip. His body was identified by his father-in-law and said he was 28 years of age. The portal said Tom and the Echovox said Bill. Shayna also picked up on a Billy. On our 2nd investigation the portal said Billy.

In 1909 Signor Pepi built the hippodrome at Bishop Auckland. The hippodrome was declared bankrupt in 1911. Signor Reni Pepi was born in 1872 in Florence, Italy.

He was renowned across all Europe as one of the three greatest quick-change artistes. He married Mary, Countess de Rossetti, a widow who was half-Italian and half-Irish. Mary died in 1915 at the age of 46. Rino Pepi died in November 1927, aged 55 years. They had made a handsome couple, he in his top hat and black flowing coat, she, in her ballgown carrying her favourite Pekinese in her arms. The dog died at the age of 11 and is buried in the walls of the Hippodrome theatre, Darlington. Did we communicate with Signor Pepi? He was a Roman Catholic and the portal said Catholic on our first visit.

In the 1911 census, Thomas Brown lived at 9 Great Gates with is wife Elizabeth Isabella, and daughters Amelia and Amanda. On the 2nd visit we got an EVP saying Amanda and the portal said Amanda too.

In the 1911 census, William Bainbridge, aged 62, fitter, Jane Bainbridge, aged 63, George Bainbridge, aged 32, butcher, John Bainbridge, Cartwright, Minnie Bainbridge, aged 25, dressmaker and Isabel Bainbridge, aged 19, (no employment listed) lived at Peel Street. The portal said Jack which is a nickname for John.

In the 1911 census, Joseph Ledgwick, aged 52, widower, groom and Stephen Place Ledgwick, aged 31, army pensioner lived at 6 Peel Street. The portal said Stephen on the 2nd investigation.

In the 1911 census, Joseph William, aged 72, feast and eggs importer, Mary Jane William, aged 72, Jasper Joseph

William, aged 33, importer son working from home, Mabel Williams, aged 39, and Rachel Knotts, aged 16, domestic servant lived at 4 Peel Street. The portal said Rachel.

In the 1911 census, Charles Dickson, aged 48, bricklayer, Mary Dickson, aged 50, Arthur Dickson, aged 13, school, Stanley Harry Victor Hyatt, aged 23, commercial Advertising Agent lived at 3 Peel Street.

In the 1911 census, Francis Edward Snailham, aged 32, fruiterer, Ruth Snailham, aged 32, Agnes Snailham, aged 9 lived at 2 Peel Street. The portal said Fran or Frank and Ted on the 2nd investigation. It also said Agnes.

In the 1911 census, John Pearson, aged 40, a jewellery dealer, Alice Pearson, aged 42, house keeper and assistant and Sarah Pearson, aged 19, servant, lived at South Church Lane. The portal said Alice and Jack.

In the 1911 census, Alise Stuart Lindsay, aged 21, a cartman lived at South Church Road. The portal said Alice.

In November 1913, there was an advert about Mr T. Hilton, at Peel Street and Railway Street.

In the 1911 census summary book these are listed:-

Timber works, T Hilton

Mineral water works, E. W. Lamb

Fruit Warehouse, J. J. Snailham

Stable and Coach house, G Cummins

6 Peel Street Private house J. Sedgewick

Workshop, J. H. Moffitt

Shop and Garage, A. Hartburn & Co

Stables, J. Mascall

4 Peel Street, private house, J. William

3 Peel Street, private house, C Dixon

2 Peel Street, private house, J. Smailham

Warehouse, empty

Workshop, A. Johnson

Fried Fish Shop, A Robson,

Fruit Warehouse, A. Hutchinson

Joiners Shop, J & W Gibson

Joinery Works, T. Manners

Office, J & R. Mascall

Warehouse, Ferrens

Timber Sheds and Stables, T. Manners

Warehouse, W & G. L. Dobson

Barracks, Salvation Army

Timber Works, T. Hilton

Fish curing works, A. Surbes

Engineers Yard and Stable, R. Charlton

Fruit Warehouse, Hart Brothers

Fruit Warehouse, J. Jarret

Hay Warehouse, W. Hind

Vulcan Hotel, Mr Williamson

In August 1916 J. J. Snailham was a wholesale fruit, flower, and potato salesman and commission agent.

In the 1939 Register, William Sheriff Snr was listed at the Vulcan Hotel with Lillian Sheriff (domestic) and William Sheriff who was at school. Minnie Bainbridge, unpaid domestic duties, George B Bainbridge, butcher and John W. Bainbridge, wheel right heavy worker also lived there. Hannah picked up on George and a butcher. The portal said Jack.

Also in the 1939 Register, Amanda Forbes was listed at Priory Grove and was listed as incarcerated. The portal mentioned prison and Amanda along with an EVP on our 2nd investigation.

The Vulcan hotel was next door at 11 Peel Street and later became a cycle shop. It was a local for the nearby trade. It was the home of Bishop Auckland Rugby Cub for a while.

I couldn't find a Garden Row at Bishop Auckland, but in the census I did find one at Sunniside, Tow Law and Broompark. Where they talking about one of these places nearby?

STAN LAUREL

The Eden Theatre originally opened in 1865 as the Masonic Music Hall, a melodrama theatre. The original architect is unknown. It underwent alterations by architect W.V. Thompson in 1871, re-opening as a 1,000 seat theatre on 28th August 1871. It was re-named Theatre Royal in 1874.

In 1892, it was leased by Arthur Jefferson (father of comedian Stan Laurel) and he employed noted theatre architect Frank Matcham to make alterations. It re-opened as the Eden Theatre, named after a well-known local family, whose son was to become Prime Minister of Great Britain in 1955-1957, Sir Anthony Eden. The seating capacity was now for 1,550 in stalls, dress circle and balcony. The Theatre Tavern on the corner of the site was incorporated into the building when further alterations were carried out by architect F.H. Liversey in 1901, and it re-opened on 24th December 1902 with a pantomime "Cinderella".

The Eden Theatre was the main theatre in Bishop Auckland for many years, but it did have some use as a cinema. It was taken over by the Newcastle based Essoldo group of cinemas in 1947, and they continued to operate the building mainly as a theatre, with some cinema use and for a short while as a bingo club.

The Eden Theatre was closed on 8th July 1961. It re-opened on 14th January 1962 and finally closed on 31st

August 1963. It then became a bingo club until 1969. It then remained empty and unused for five years. It was demolished in 1974 for a road widening scheme. Today there is a plaque on a wall commemorating the site of the theatre. There is also a statue of Stan Laurel where the theatre once stood.

Stan Laurel was christened Arthur Stanley Jefferson at Bishop Auckland along with his sister.

Stan wrote a letter to a childhood friend in 1960 and in it he said that he used to ride his pony on the sands at Tynemouth. Stans pony was called Peggy. Hannah picked up on the name Peggy at Labyrinth.

The portal also said 'Bob' at both Greggs and Labyrinth, which was the name of Stan's son who died at only 9 days old. The portal also said 'Arthur' a few times at Cre8ive graphics, which was Stan's first Name and the name of his father.

The portal said 'from Sid' at Cre8ive graphics. Stan's brother was called Sydney Everitt Jefferson and when he was less than 5 months old.

Oliver Hardy was Stan's onscreen partner. The portal said Oliver at Cre8ive graphics. Stan was a member of Fred Kamo's Army, where he was Charlie Chaplins understudy.

Charlie Chaplin was born in South London. A man with a Cockney accent came through the portal at Cre8ive Graphics. The portal also said Hannah twice at Cre8ive Graphics and Charlie Chaplin's mother was called Hannah.

Hannah had an illegitimate son called Sydney and the portal also said Sid.

Between 1916 and 1918, Stan teamed up with Alice and Baldwin Cooke to become the Stan Jefferson Trio. The portal said Alice at Cre8ive Graphics.

Trenton is the capital city of the U.S. state of New Jersey. Jean Acker, an American actress was from Trenton. She was married to Rudolph Valentino. He was referenced in the film Mud and Sand, a parody of Blood and Sand, which starred Stan Laurel as a bullfighter named Rhubarb Vaseline. The portal said Trenton at Cre8ive Graphics.

APPENDIX

The spirit Box – A tool for generating white noise for spirit to communicate. It uses radio frequency.

The Portal – A device that is used with the spirit box. It is a device that enhances EVP as it reduces the radio signal. It enhances the sound, allowing the words to be heard more clearly.

EVP (Electronic voice phenomenon) –Sounds found on electronic recordings that are interpreted as spirit voices.

Orbs or Light Anomalies –A ball of light caused by spirit energy. A true orb with have a face, number or letter within it when zoomed in. You have to be really careful as dust particles and moisture can easily be mistaken for obs.

Table tipping –A type of séance in which participants sit around a table, place their hands on it and wait for spirit to move, rotate or lift the table.

K2 Meter – A gadget that detects spikes in electromagnetic energy. These spikes indicated by the lights signify activity or communication from the spirit world. You need to test the area for cables and electrical equipment as these also give off electromagnetic energy.

Poppy bear – this works the same as the K2 meter but the paws light up Green and Red. This is popular with spirit children.

Handy Cam – A small hand held camcorder that can film in the dark.

Full Spectrum Camera – A specially adapted camera that detects more light than a normal camera. It is able to capture infrared images, ultraviolet light images and much more.

Thermal imaging Camera – A camera that detects heat and cold spots by showing them up in different colours in the photo.

Ovilus/Talker2 – Converts environmental readings into real words. Theories suggest that spirit may be able to choose words from a pre-set database of over 2000 words.

Rempod – A device that detects spirit, it has lights and sound that activates when a spirit it close. Because the REM pod radiates its own field it can detect much more, which in theory makes it easier for spirits to communicate.

SLS (structured light sensor) Kinect camera uses sensors to detect movement and when connect to a laptop or tablet it uses those sensors to draw out a stickman figure.

ACKNOWLEDGEMENTS

A huge thankyou to Bish Vegas Legal Graff who have allowed me to use their fabulous mural of Stan Laurel. Stan Laurel went to school at King James 1st and lived at Princes Street so it seemed very fitting to have this fabulous tribute on the cover of the book.

We think that we may have linked to Stan Laurel at Cre8ive Graphics. Stan is also featured on our 2nd book.

The members of Bish Vegas Legal Graff are Dan Walls, www.illuminationwallart.co.uk, Michael David Clarke, Instagram theputrideye, and Raven Nelson-Flower, Instagram rheyyahntattoo or find her at Sakura Tattoo at Gosforth.

Check out their other work around the town!

Every effort has been made as to the names and dates in this book. Errors and omissions excepted (E&OE). All information was gathered through mediumship and cannot, therefore, be proven in any way, therefore must be used for entertainment purposes only.